CHAKRAS FOR BEGINNERS

*How to Awaken and Balance Chakras,
and Radiate Positive Energy and Heal Yourself*

TABLE OF CONTENTS

INTRODUCTION 1

CHAPTER 1: CHAKRAS AND YOU 3

CHAPTER 2: THE CENTERS OF CONSCIOUSNESS THROUGH TIME 21

CHAPTER 3: CHAKRAS AND THE EVOLUTION OF HUMAN CONSCIOUSNESS – PART 1 23

CHAPTER 3B: CHAKRAS AND THE EVOLUTION OF HUMAN CONSCIOUSNESS - PART 2 33

CHAPTER 4: THE BENEFIT OF THE DIFFERENT CHAKRAS 44

CHAPTER 5: AWAKENING YOUR SEVEN CHAKRAS 51

　　1. Root Chakra: 51

　　2 & 3. Navel Center Chakra: 51

　　4. Heart Chakra: 52

　　5. Throat Chakra: 52

　　6. Third Eye: 52

　　7. Crown Chakra: 52

CHAPTER 6: CHAKRAS, ENDOCRINE SYSTEM AND THE IMMUNE SYSTEM 57

CHAPTER 7: CHAKRAS AND PLANETS 67

CHAPTER 8: PROBLEMS THAT SOME OF THE CHAKRAS MAY ENCOUNTER 75

CHAPTER 9: REMEDIES FOR DAMAGED CHAKRAS.....79

CHAPTER 10: CRYSTAL HEALING FOR CHAKRAS........90

CHAPTER 11: USING JOURNALING TO SPEAK THE TRUTH AND HELP YOUR THROAT CHAKRA 95

CHAPTER 12: HOW TO PRACTICE LOVE FOR YOURSELF AND OTHERS TO OPEN UP THE HEART CHAKRA 99

CHAPTER 13: THE EFFECT OF YOGA ON CHAKRAS ..105

CHAPTER 14: USING MEDITATION TO HELP YOUR CHAKRAS..109

CHAPTER 15: VISUALIZATION OF YOUR CHAKRAS..115

CHAPTER 16: OTHER REMEDIES FOR YOUR CHAKRAS..121

CHAPTER 16B: OTHER REMEDIES FOR YOUR CHAKRAS PART 2..125

CHAPTER 17: THE 12-CHAKRA SYSTEM – PART 1........135

CHAPTER 17B: THE 12-CHAKRA SYSTEM – PART 2.....143

CHAPTER 18: QUESTIONS FOR SELF-EXAMINATION 154

CHAPTER 19: THE SCIENCE BEHIND CHAKRAS.........161

CHAPTER 20: AS ABOVE, SO BELOW 172

CONCLUSION 181

<u>Claim Your FREE</u>
<u>Meditation & Yoga Bonus Gift</u>

INTRODUCTION

I want to thank you and congratulate you for reading the book, "Chakras for Beginners - How to Awaken Your Chakras, Balance Chakras, and Radiate Positive Energy."

This book contains steps and strategies on how to awaken your chakras, how to balance these energies emanating from the chakra points in your body, and how to use this knowledge to make your life better.

For over a thousand years, many people have been interested in psychic studies, not only for paranormal pursuits but for health benefits as well. Knowing your chakra points will definitely give you an edge in balancing your life, making better decisions and generally living a healthier life; the gift of seeing and feeling these chakra points in action is a bonus.

Energy radiates from our chakras. When you are happy or angry, psychics will be able to see a colored light surrounding you. The color may be red, blue, or white, depending on the emotions you feel that day. The stronger the emotions you feel, the stronger the light will be. On the other hand, your chakra points may also weaken, especially if you have an illness. This is why you can use crystals or gemstones for healing. You actually place them on your chakra points and the positive energy carried by the crystals will then be transferred to the chakra points.

1

Ultimately, the chakra points are the basis for any other psychic link and activity. For instance, a person with an active third eye (otherwise known as the sixth sense) has the crown chakra working properly and actively, too. People who can read auras will be able to see the purple light coming above your head and enveloping your whole body. Thus, it is important to note the different chakra points in the body and how you can balance the energy coming from them.

This book will teach you exactly that. This gem contains all the things that you need to know about chakras – the chakra points, the strengths and weaknesses of each point, the colors, notes and gemstones that you can equip yourself with and, more importantly, how to awaken and balance your chakras so that one point is not overpowered by the other. Learn real stuff from this book and see how you can manifest and radiate positive energy through your chakras.

Thanks again for reading this book, I hope you enjoy it!

CHAPTER 1:

CHAKRAS AND YOU

Your chakras are an integral part of your daily life. While many people don't realize what is going on in their bodies, most of the time your chakras are the parts that control this. When things seem to be wrong in the body, like you feel overwhelmed or have trouble talking to other people, your chakras may be the reason that you are dealing with this. On the other hand, when you feel really good about your life, you feel like you are able to talk to other people, love other people and you don't feel like things are wrong, your chakras are most likely aligned together.

Knowledge of the chakras and how you can strengthen them is vital to your overall physical, mental and spiritual health. Chakras are typically defined as the (sometimes) invisible force fields around you, which emanate positive or negative energies depending on your mood, emotions and health status.

The history of chakras goes back a long way. Starting in the 7th century BCE, the Hindus produced texts linking the deities, religious canon and the knowledge of these psychic force fields. During this time, the Hindus recorded and wrote the Upanishads – the tome of sacred texts that contained the beliefs of Hindus. Aside from learning about karma and reincarnation, practitioners and then readers of the Upanishads knew that the body had various energy points. Moreover, it claimed that the soul settled in different parts of the body.

Understanding Chakras will have you going back to the beginning of time. It is said that the real birthplace of the human race was in Tanzania, and a certain Mount Meru, also known as a mystical mountain is located here. Mount Meru is believed to be where the Goddess Shri Lalita, who was the main source of the nine interlocking triangles—or chakras— used to reside. She represents the union of the masculine and feminine and also symbolizes the intersection of power from different parts of the body.

The chakras are so important to your body. Even if just one of the chakras is badly aligned, you will notice that all of them can become blocked and not working that well. All of the chakras need to have energy flowing through them properly so if one of the chakras doesn't allow the energy to flow through, there are going to be some big problems that arise. You need to learn how to let the energy flow through the chakras to help them to feel better and this can be done in no time at all.

When the chakras are opened up, you will notice that you feel so much better than ever before. Opened chakras allow you to talk to others, open up your heart to others, feel grounded in the world around you, and even to have a connection to a higher power. All of these can be important to live a happy and healthy life. In many cases, our modern world makes it really difficult to keep the chakras working as well as you would like them to. We are too stressed out, we are worried about keeping our jobs and we may not have much of a chance to open up to some other people. It does take some active work to help keep the chakras as open up as possible.

When the chakras are closed up, you will quickly notice that there can be issues that arise as a result of this. You may feel shy when you are with other people. You may not be able to show or share the love with some of the other people in your life, or you may not be able to stay grounded in the life that you have. There are so many elements of your life that can go wrong when you are dealing with your chakras not working properly and if one of the chakras is out of order, and not letting through the energy that you need, all of them can begin to fail pretty quickly.

Another problem that you may have is that a chakra will allow in too much energy compared to what it should. For example, if your throat chakra is open too much, you may blurt out anything that comes into your head, even if it isn't necessary or will cause a lot of pain to someone else when you don't need to do this. When the throat chakra is working properly, you will find that it works well to help you show honesty and speak up properly, so you don't want it to let in too much and say a lot of things that are not necessary and could cause issues with other people.

Working on the chakras is one of the best things that you can do for your overall health. It allows you to improve your life better than ever before because you get the chance to understand how all of the chakras work together and how they influence the different parts of your life. When you are able to get them to work together well, you will notice a huge improvement in your life in no time.

Mount Meru also signifies one's journey from the start or

bottom of his life, all the way to the top, which shows where chakras and the energy system began.

Back in India

The thing about Mount Meru is that it also appears in both Indian and Egyptian Mythology, which coincides with the Vedas, known as the oldest written Indian traditions. This dates back to 1,500 to 500 B.C.

The Vedas are recorded from the Brahmins Caste. They entered India from the North and propagated Aryan stock as a means of gratitude to Shri Lalita. The term "Chakra" was then born.

The Brahma Upanishads, for instance, taught Hindus that there are four important places in the body where the soul resides: the head, throat, heart and the navel. Further, the texts stated that your waking consciousness is found in the navel; dreamless sleep is found in the heart; dreaming is found in the throat, and the transcendent state is in the head.

The Yogattatva Upanishads, on the other hand, said that the body parts were associated with the elements of fire, air, water, earth, and ether. It is clear that even in the sacred texts, the body is described to coexist with psychic elements. Thus, the body is not simply a vessel, but it is an extension of the world's energies.

Anyone who has seen auras will say that these auras have colors and different vibrations. Where they come from – the chakra points – also influence the kind of auras that people see in you. If you feel very happy or excited, your aura will manifest the energy that you feel; such energy can even be transferred to other people. Have you ever walked into a room full of angry people, only to leave the same room feeling angry yourself? That is the aura and energy at work. You somehow absorb the energy, whether positive or negative, emanating from other people.

Originally, chakra denotes the meaning of "wheels" which symbolized *chakravartins*, or the chariot wheels of rulers. It was also used as a metaphor for the sun. Ancient Hindus believed that the sun could traverse the world like the most triumphant and skilled chariot. It also represents balance and eternal order, more than anything in the world.

Sometimes, chakras get damaged too, as you'll learn in some of the chapters of this book, which means that, like people, they're not always in their best state. This fact also makes them more real—and is one of the reasons why you have to learn about them and pay attention to them.

With the birth of chakras came the dawn of a new age. According to the old writings, the new age symbolized Christ's halo as it was preceded by a golden disk of light. This also signified the emergence of Vishnu, one of the three main deities of Hinduism. Vishnu is often referred to as the *Protector* or the *Preserver.* Vishnu is said to have descended from the earth, holding a conch shell, a lotus flower, a cakra and a club in his four arms. Cakra is said to be a weapon that resembled a discus.

The way you feel also affects your health. Scientific studies prove that feeling sorrowful and depressed can be linked to serious illnesses such as fatigue, cancer and heart problems. Joyous people may have illnesses, too, but these may not be as serious or fatal as those perpetually sad people have.

The work of the chakras is evident here. When your chakras are active and balanced, you will be able to manifest positive energy and vibrantly colored auras. Your moods are uplifted and you feel happy all the time. You don't feel pain or any illness. The more awakened and balanced your chakras are, the better it will be for your body.

Knowing how chakras works are beneficial to your emotional health as well. Imbalanced chakras are like imbalanced hormones. You feel weak, and you don't have much control over your emotions. When you know how to deal with your chakra points and use other psychic forms of self-healing, your emotional state will be much better. You won't have mood swings; instead, you will immediately be able to block negative forces and emotional baggage that will try to pull you down.

The Seven Chakras of your Body

The word chakra means "wheel of light." This is true because when people see your aura, they see lights in different colors cocooning you. These chakras are conduits of earth and cosmic energies and connect all the seven layers of your aura. There are energies that come forth from the chakra points.

The chakra points are connected to the various parts of the body. Your body has seven main chakras, and 2 extra chakras that just come up every once in a while. Your seven main chakras are ones that you should focus on because they affect your mood as they are connected to systems in your body.

They also have a variety of states, depending on the flow of energy in your body. The Chakras may be open, blocked or sealed. Open chakras radiate more energy. As such, your body becomes more sensitive and receptive to healing and balancing. During the beginning of a healing session, whether it is through acupuncture, crystal healing or reiki, your chakra points must be open to the energies that will be transferred to you.

In contrast, there are chakras that are sealed. This means that there is a layer that protects your chakras. This is healthy, too, because the layers prevent negative forces from coming in. Think of this as a mantra for some people. Whenever they don't want to feel down or angry, they say a mantra to quickly protect themselves from being influenced by outside forces. They say affirmations like "I will be happy today" or "I can feel that my day will be alright." This is a form of meditation and a way to seal your chakra points.

The Chakras may also be blocked, meaning energy is not flowing properly at one point. Blocked chakras affect other chakra points and cause imbalance. Thus, it is important that you have your chakras opened during your meditative state.

A balanced and healthy chakra will be able to radiate positive energy and the right amount of energy at that. The energy flows freely, but it will not overpower and block your other chakra points. The point of this book is to teach you how to awaken your chakras and manage them to prevent any imbalance of energy in your body.

As aforementioned, there are seven chakras in your body. These chakra points help you in different aspects – physical health, emotions, psychic abilities, etc. These chakras are:

The Earth Star Chakra

The earth star connects you to the elemental energies of the earth. It helps to anchor you to the earth plane so you will be more grounded and logical. Though you acknowledge yourself as a Being of the Light, you have to ground yourself, too, to avoid any misguided feelings. You also need to be grounded so that you can participate in your present embodiment. It helps you remember your highest path in life, your highest affirmations.

The earth star chakra is located beneath your feet. The colors associated with the earth star chakra are silver, black and maroon. Naturally, you could choose gemstones and crystals with these colors to aid you in your psychic healing. These stones are onyx, hematite, tiger's eye and garnet. In terms of psychic ability, you will know how to ground yourself and align yourself with the wonderful powers of the earth.

The good thing about strengthening your earth star chakra is that you become conscious of your being and that you know you are a spirit manifesting itself on the physical plane. You will display a passion and zest for life, and you know how to detach yourself from the chains of the past and the uncertainties of the future. The shadows or weaknesses related to the earth star chakra are depression or disconnection from relationships, lack of motivation to do your activities, and disorders associated with immunity. Hence, you need to activate your earth star chakra to protect yourself from getting anxious and lazy.

The Root Chakra

The root chakra is the source of your usable physical energy and anchors this energy into your physical manifestation. This region is in charge of family and survival issues, relationships, especially within a group. It is the foundation for all the aspects and qualities of your physical being. It is located at the base of your spine that spirals towards the earth star chakra. The color linked to it is red, and the element is earth. In music, the note related to the root chakra is the G below middle C.

This represents the feeling of being grounded and is deemed

to be the foundation of all chakras. It is located in the tailbone area of the spine and is related to issues of survival (hunger, financial, etc.).

When the root chakra is strong, your abilities to touch and smell are strong as well. Likewise, you become clairsentient. Your olfactory senses also work as a psychic ability. This means you can smell and feel unseen entities while others who are not that sensitive and whose root chakras aren't active won't be able to notice any difference in the ambiance of a place.

To complement the energies coming from your root chakra, it is best to wear or bring the following gemstones for protection, healing, and extra motivation: ruby, bloodstone, smoky quartz, obsidian, tourmaline, garnet, red jasper and red quartz. Naturally, the colors that you have to look for are red and black. Your root chakra is also responsible for the healing of your skeletal system and circulatory system, your bladder, kidneys, rectum, hips, adrenal gland, skin, feet, and legs. When used properly, the root chakra will help you understand that all things are connected. You become more grounded and stronger when facing uncertainty. You also feel that you belong to a certain place or group. You are more secure and nurturing, channeling the Mother archetype.

When you feel an imbalance in the energy, you feel like giving up and are unable to cope. You also feel that you want to detach yourself from a group. You exclude others and you adopt a superior stance. You also channel the Victim archetype and tend to think that everyone is against you. You also feel so insecure.

The Sacral Chakra

Next is the Sacral Chakra, which is located in the lower abdomen and denotes one's ability to experience adventures and connect with others. It is also related to the sense of pleasure, well-being, abundance, and sexuality.

This chakra is responsible for your emotions and how you relate to others. It is likewise associated with creativity and sexual energy. This chakra point helps you interpret and understand others by looking within yourself. It also recognizes the duality of yin and yang that there are opposing forces and how you can deal with them properly. Doing so helps you heal emotionally. When you activate the sacral chakra, you become better at handling your finances and you are able to use your creativity for your business and hobbies. You also become better at understanding your partner in bed.

Located a few inches below the navel, the sacral chakra is associated with the color orange. Gemstones of such hue are coral, carnelian, and amber, all of which boost your inner drive to finish your projects and work on other things creative such as art and fiction. In terms of music, the note related to the sacral chakra is D, just above middle C. You are akin to the water element, and you have a stronger ability to taste or touch. Likewise, you are able to smell unseen entities, and you easily connect with people. You have an ability to empathize and absorb whatever feelings other people have. Opening your sacral chakra can be helpful if you have problems in the lower back, reproductive organs, lymphatic system, kidneys, bladder and large intestine.

An active sacral chakra will allow you to embody integrity and respect in a relationship. You also become a highly creative individual, focusing on enjoyment, pleasure, and sensuality. You also channel the Empress archetype, a queen who is always in her element.

On not so good days, you might channel the Martyr archetype. You are moody, manipulative, and you deny yourself pleasure. You have a tendency to get addicted, too. You feel more guilt and fear.

The Solar Plexus Chakra

Located in the upper abdomen, this denotes a person's ability to be in control of his life, and to be confident, as well. It also deals with issues of self-esteem and self-worth. In short, when this chakra is damaged, you might feel bad about yourself, and it really will affect your mood and your day.

The solar plexus empowers your self-esteem and gives you a higher sense of self. It strengthens the honor and integrity that you feel. However, the solar plexus chakra also seeks not only your own empowerment but others as well.

This chakra relates to your mental energy because it gives you the capability to make decisions well. It connects you with your intuition. It likewise ensures that you can handle your emotional energies very well.

The solar plexus is located below the sternum and two inches above the navel. The color it connects to is yellow, the musical note is F, and the natural element is fire. An active and healthy solar plexus chakra means you have a keen sense of sight and your gut instincts are working and accurate. For accessories, use the gemstones: gold topaz, citrine, amber, gold calcite, tiger's eyes, orange quartz or any crystal with yellow or gold color.

When you feel any ailment in the digestive system, activating the solar plexus chakra will help you a lot. Specifically, it heals your gallbladder, stomach, small intestine, liver, and pancreas. A balanced solar plexus chakra means you treat yourself with integrity and respect. You have a strong sense of confidence. You are self-disciplined, generous and brave. You honor your ambition, yet make clear decisions. You have a gut level intuition and good ethics. You know your self-worth. You know where to direct all your energy. You are a Warrior.

In contrast, you could also have low self-esteem, you may lack personal identity, and you give too much even when you don't have to. You may also be narcissistic and may need constant reassurance. Thus, you become the Servant archetype.

The Heart Chakra

As the name suggests, this has a lot to do with a person's ability to love and is located just above the heart, in the center of one's chest. It deals with joy, peace, love, and healing.

This chakra focuses on love, forgiveness, and compassion. Whatever emotional pain you feel becomes a catalyst and you find yourself transformed by circumstances. The heart chakra houses humanitarian care. Because it is the center of your body, it focuses on love as the basis of living. This chakra is located just above the heart and is associated with the colors pink and green. The musical note is G, and your element is air. You have a sensitive sense of touch and your psychic abilities are clairsentience and psychometry. Wear gemstones that are pink or green: unakite, rose quartz, moss agate, emerald, green jade, aventurine, and tourmaline. You may also wear malachite.

The heart chakra helps your respiratory system. This includes your lungs, heart and your diaphragm. As suggested by the name, the mantra that you can tell yourself is that love is the highest power. Above all, love is the highest form of respect and care that you could give to yourself and to others. You feel love, forgiveness, hope, compassion for other people, dedication, divine inspiration, peace, kindness, and humor. You feel light and you have the ability to connect with others on an emotional level. Channeling the lover archetype, you can definitely feel what others need.

In contrast, you may also feel bouts of anger and jealousy. Resentment will bubble to the surface, and you may have a hard time forgiving others. You may become secretive and alienate yourself from other people. This is otherwise known as the Actor archetype.

The Thymus Chakra

This chakra takes you into the realm of unconditional love. You are showered with divine light, wisdom, and healing. Everything is clear to you, and you are more open to others. You accept people for who they are. The thymus chakra is the gateway to the highest life path, and it is where your intent is born. When you are angry, the thymus chakra tries to stop you from saying something that you will regret later on. You become more attuned to the higher levels of consciousness and your dreams and ambitions.

The thymus chakra is located between your throat chakra and your heart. The wellspring of energy, the thymus chakra is associated with the colors aqua, green and purple. The thymus chakra is also related to the endocrine system, the thymus gland, and the immune system. White fire is your element.

For gemstones, it is best that you choose lapis lazuli, aquamarine, azurite, and turquoise. In terms of psychic ability, you are capable of lucid dreaming, while you believe that love is your highest intent. You have the power to be open to others, and it is easy for you to express your emotions to people. It is also easy for you to express your love to those you care for. You have aspirations and love for divine light. You can easily realize your dreams and you know how to make them come true.

When the thymus chakra is blocked, you don't have that much power in yourself. Thus, you are easily manipulated by people. You reject spirituality and the help of others. You become closed to advice yourself, and you are unable to express your feelings. It is either you feel you are judged quickly, or you judge others without giving them enough merit.

The Throat Chakra

This helps you express yourself and communicate your message properly. You become more creative, and you have the willpower and the choice to make healthy decisions. You live up to your personal honor. The throat chakra connects your mind and your heart. Located in the throat, this denotes one's ability to communicate and is also related to the truth and feelings of self-expression. If this is damaged, you may have all these bottled-up feelings inside—feelings that might affect your day, and your life, when not attended to.

This chakra is like a teacher who tells you the truth about her soul. She opens up space for you to experience wisdom. You share the wonderful experience that penetrates the soul and elevates yourself to a higher plane of existence. The throat chakra is where your soul's expression is. Located at the base of your throat, the chakra helps you exercise willpower, as this is the sustenance of the soul. Without it, your soul is but a shadow that resides in a physical vessel.

The color best associated with the throat chakra is sky blue while the note is A. Your element is ether or space. You have a clear and astute sense of hearing. You also have the ability to hear spirits and taste colors and experience (not just food). You have a good sense of smell and speaking to unseen forces (thus, you can become a séance). You are able to communicate using your mind. This is called telepathy.

The gemstones that you need are amazonite, sodalite, aquamarine, lapis lazuli, and turquoise. Blue is not just the color of the intellect, but it is also the color of confidence, communication, and wisdom. Use the throat chakra to heal your thyroid gland, teeth, mouth, throat, neck, voice, and tongue. Your personal mantra is merged your personal will with the Divine will.

You have the power to uplift yourself through self-expression. You can speak what your soul wants to say, your message as clear as the water that runs into the river. You know how to get to what makes you really happy.

The throat chakra makes you clairaudient and telepathic. You are the Communicator archetype. On low days, you are inarticulate, you become critical of what others do, and your tongue is as sharp as a sword. You lash out at others, and you may lack the willpower to change or address a problem using the best solution. You may even be wont to lie and distort the truth. That, or you may be uncooperative because you are channeling the Silent Child archetype.

The Third Eye Chakra

This denotes one's ability to focus and see the bigger picture and is located between the eyes in the forehead. It is also related to one's ability to think, wisdom and intuition.

This is the center of your visions, your intellect, and your intuition. If you have the ability to see and talk to spirits, your third eye is at work. Unlike the average person, you are more sensitive to sounds, motion and other happenings that may not be perceived in this world, but are possible only in paranormal studies. The brow chakra, as it is called, is where your psychic abilities are found and honed.

The third eye chakra is where you find and evaluate your insights. It gains wisdom from everything that you have experienced. When you allow your third eye to work, you trust a higher power and you begin to align yourself with the powers that you don't see.

The chakra is located in the center of your forehead, between your brows, thus the name brow chakra. The color that emanates from this region is violet or indigo blue, and the gemstones best associated with it are amethyst, fluorite and lapis lazuli. The musical note is D, and the element is spiritual energy. You are gifted with inner knowledge and you know yourself fully. You also have the gift of telepathy, astral projection, and clairvoyance. The third eye chakra works well with the head, the brain, the whole nervous system, the eyes, skull, pituitary gland, and all of your sense organs. The mantra is to seek only the highest truth, although this will be dependent on what you believe to be the highest truth.

The power that governs you is the power to focus on your life. The powers of your imagination are heightened, and you are more aware of your past life. You embody the Wise Person archetype.

However, there will be times when you feel so bored and uninterested in the things that you normally do. You become judgmental and overly critical of people. You tend to think too much and you lack the imagination to create things. Thus, the Wise Person self is transformed into the Intellectual, and you dismiss intuition.

The Crown Chakra

This is located on top of the head and is also related to one's connection with his spirituality, together with inner and outer beauty.

The crown chakra unifies or connects you with the Higher Self and your spiritual consciousness. The crown chakra opens and connects you to higher dimensions, making you an enlightened individual. This is the highest and most important of all the chakras in the body. Located at the top of your head, the color that comes from the crown chakras is gold, white or purple. The musical note is G, and the elements are photon and cosmic energies. When this spot is active, your spiritual awareness is awakened and you are attuned to the universe. You live in the present, and you have no emotional baggage that ties you to the past. You know when to let go.

Your psychic abilities include telepathy, claircognizance, and channeling. The best gemstones for you are selenite and clear quartz. You can heal the pain in some parts of your spinal cord, brain, and the pineal gland. You are the Guru archetype.

When you are weak, this shifts to the Egoist archetype, who is materialistic, dogmatic and depressed.

The Soul Star Chakra

This chakra is filled with intense light that it is reflected in other chakra points. The soul star is responsible for the incarnation of the soul. It also provides spiritual energies for your soul, so that you are reminded of your destiny and purpose. The soul star is situated above your head, and the color that comes from it is white. The gemstones perfect for this purpose are Lemurian seed crystals and selenite. You can connect with God and you know that you have a higher purpose in this world.

CHAPTER 2:

THE CENTERS OF CONSCIOUSNESS THROUGH TIME

The Upanishads began the teachings of chakras that are still being used and adhered to up to today, which are often called the Centers of Consciousness. This started in 600 BC, and the teachings were adopted by the Yoga Sutras of Patanjali in 200 BC.

Chakras are known to be the centers of consciousness mostly because they say a lot about how you feel, how your day will be, and how your emotions are going to play a role in your life.

Chakras in Patanjali were said to interpret:

1. Pure Consciousness (Purusha)
2. Prima Materia of the World (Prakriti)

They believed that by doing yoga, one can awaken his chakras, and rise above plain consciousness, in order to realize pure consciousness. This way, the mind will not fluctuate just because of emotions, especially anger and loneliness. This will also invoke a higher and much deeper kind of synthesis for you.

The Rise of Chakra System and Kundalini Yoga

The Tantric Tradition then gave way to the rise of chakra, with the help of Kundalini Yoga. This happened in the Common Era, also known as the second half of the first millennium.

Tantra literally means "tool for stretching," which made people believe that by doing yoga exercises, they'll be able to tap into their chakras. However, it all started as a sexual tradition, but over the years, these practices were also used to give recognition to deities and goddesses. By doing so, one is believed to be able to integrate the universe's many polaric forces.

The 1900s to Today

In 1919, the first manuscript that's believed to explain chakras was introduced to the West by a man named Arthur Avalon. This book was entitled *The Serpent Power*. In the said book, he was able to explain various practices that people did—and can do—to awaken the chakras, including the ways one has to meditate in order to tap into various chakras. This is called *Gorakshashatakam*, which is now deemed as the precursor of today's Chakra theory, together with Tantric Sex, and Kundalini Yoga.

CHAPTER 3:

CHAKRAS AND THE EVOLUTION OF HUMAN CONSCIOUSNESS – PART 1

After discussing chakras for so long now, you are clear that there are 7 primary chakras or energy points arranged in a straight line right from the base of the spine to the crown of the head. All thoughts, emotions, and intentions are all registered as energy in the relevant chakras. As time passes, your focus and your level of consciousness in your life are two critical factors that decide how effectively energy flows through these nodes.

Weak energy flow translates to an individual who leads a scattered, unfocused, and unconscious way of life while a strong energy flow translates to a person who is aware, focused, and highly conscious of every moment in his life. Energy is the power behind the creation and maintenance of this entire universe. Therefore, the way we manage our energies decides how powerful and strong our life forces will play out.

Your physical body reflects your internal state of mind. Your physical body will align itself automatically to how you are feeling; whether sad or happy, clear or confused, joyful or scared, anxious or expectant, etc. This book has already covered how every chakra is associated with a particular location, color, organs/glands, etc.

The next few chapters are dedicated to giving you insights about the connection between chakras and the various levels of consciousness along with some tips and ideas on how to activate the chakras to activate the consciousness level associated with it. The higher you are able to climb the ladder of consciousness, the closer you are to achieving spiritual unity with the universe. So, here goes the 7 levels of consciousness linked to the seven chakras.

Root Chakra – the First Tier of Consciousness

Human beings are the first and the only species that was given the power of consciousness when it evolved many thousands of years ago. Until then, this concept of the consciousness was completely absent in living beings. While the initial level of consciousness was restricted to only the awareness of the physical body and the surroundings, it was still a powerful element in the process of evolution.

Although we have evolved into much higher levels of consciousness from the days of the first man on earth, even today we need these basic survival instincts and physical needs to keep our afloat. If the fundamental aspects of your life are not in order, there is no point in being aware of higher consciousness as a weak foundation can bring the entire system crashing down.

Moreover, a strong root chakra will keep you grounded and connected to reality even when you manage to achieve and reach higher levels of consciousness. A powerful ability to live well at lower frequencies will help you survive well in this highly competitive world. A point to note here is that a difficult or traumatic childhood or a deep-rooted fear of physical danger that happened earlier in your life could be a reason for a weak root chakra

The root chakra or the 'mooladhara' chakra ('mool' in Sanskrit means root or foundation) is the first the level of consciousness and is the place where the 'karmas' of our past actions (both in this life and past lives) are stored. They lie dormant in this dark space waiting to be awakened.

As this chakra is very closely linked to our physicality, the awakening of it could result in activating negative emotions such as desires, anger, hatred, etc. It is, therefore, essential to keep this chakra in a balanced state so that we are grounded well enough and yet can control active qualities.

The element associated with the root chakra is the earth which represents our deep connection to this extremely important and physical element of life. The earth is a provider of nourishment and energy and people with a robust root chakra are usually dependable, unhurried, patient, and practical.

The basic quality of the 'mooladhara' chakra is innocence and like the innocence of newborn baby finds happiness when simple physical desires are taken care of. Purity, joy, and simplicity are associated with this fundamental chakra associated with the first level of consciousness.

A person who is primarily guided by this chakra will be innocent and joyful and hardly conscious of ulterior motives. However, when other people take advantage of such people's innocent and pure life, then they can awaken to some powerful emotions that can change their personality drastically.

When this root chakra is awakened, the person's sense of smell is heightened significantly. The individual will be able to discern a wide variety of odors and smells that are not commonly discernible by those whose root chakra is not powerfully awakened.

Methods of Balancing the Root Chakra

Mantra – You can chant the mantra LUM (rhyming with 'hum') seven times each day. As you chant this mantra, imagine a spinning red wheel at the base of your spine. Affirmations such as 'I am strong,' 'I am safe,' etc can help in balancing the root chakra. These affirmations help to heal fears of insecurities.

Meditation – During your meditation times, imagine yourself powerfully and irrevocably rooted to the earth. As you feel the connection between your body and the earth, imagine the energies of Mother Earth enter via the root chakra and spread the sense of security to every cell in your body.

Diet – Vegetables such as carrots, potatoes, beets, and radishes (basically root veggies that find their own energy to grow in the womb of Mother Earth) are great to enhance the balance of your root chakra. Foods that are rich in protein such as nuts, eggs, meat, and legumes are good too. Spices that help in balancing the root chakra include hot red peppers, paprika, and chili.

Sacral Chakra – the Second Tier of Consciousness

A good analogy to explain the second tier of consciousness is to compare with a toddler. Imagine a toddler. His basic requirements of food, sleep, potty, etc are taken care of. Then, what does he do? He begins to look around at his surroundings trying to catch anything within his reach calling it his own. This is the 'identity building' level wherein the toddler is finding his ego. He is trying to come to terms with some basic emotions such as fear, joy, and anger.

At the level of human evolution, it is that stage when man realized that he can talk and communicate with other people using spoken and singing languages. Man realized that the world is a powerfully magical place where there is much to be explored. Yet, man also felt apprehension as he thought the same magical world also had plenty of things to be fearful about.

Man began to find solace and peace for his fears through the use of spells and rituals. He tried to control and appease gods, goddesses, nature through these rituals and spells. Rituals and rites became all-powerful and those who managed these rites and rituals became the kings and kingmakers. Man formed small societies and communities to feel safe and secure.

The connection between the second chakra and the second level of consciousness is that at this stage, man is conditioning and molding his society. At this level, we choose to suppress and control our basic desires and needs to 'fit into society.' At this stage, we are taught to keep a tight leash on our emotions and desires. Sadly, this results in a sense of repression and we feel disconnected with our physical self. This is what happens when the sacral chakra or the second level of consciousness is suppressed.

An open and freely flowing sacral chakra helps you live in the moment and allows the creative juices in your heart and mind to flow abundantly. A person with a balanced sacral chakra will feel comfortable with his or her feelings of intimacy, passions, and relationships.

The Sanskrit name for the sacral chakra is Svadhisthana; 'sva' means self and 'sthana' means place. The translation would be 'seat or place of the self.' This is the place where the energy of creation sits and is set in motion. Here too, the spiritual energy from our past karmas are dormant while our conventional temptations and desires drive our lives.

The element of this chakra is water and like water, this chakra represents fluidity, spontaneity, and flexibility. While fluidity and flexibility are great attitudes in some ways, they are also the reason for unpredictability. The underlying quality of this chakra is emotion and the ability to connect with emotions. The energy of this chakra is predominantly feminine. An individual who is primarily guided by the sacral chakra is creative, impulsive, and highly emotional.

The sense that guides this chakra is taste and someone who largely uses this chakra in his or her life will invariably depend on eating and the sense of taste to deal with unmanageable emotions.

Methods of Balancing the Sacral Chakra

Mantra – An effective mantra to balance your sacral chakra is 'vam' (rhyming with 'hum'). Chant this mantra seven times a day and as you chant imagine an orange (the color associated with this chakra) wheel spinning in the area beneath your navel (the position of the sacral chakra).

Affirmations such as 'I embody creativity and life,' 'I embrace the joy and passion of life,' etc can enhance the power of this chakra. These affirmations and mantras can help in healing the effects of repressed emotions.

Meditation – During meditation, place your hand on your

lower belly and imagine a healing sphere of orange light expanding in that area. Dip your emotional energy into that bright, expanding orange light and feel yourself uplifted and free from any sense of repression.

Diet – foods, and spices that nourish the sacral chakra include oranges, passion fruits, strawberries, melons, vanilla, cinnamon, and honey.

The sacral or the 'svadhisthana' chakra is a sweet place where your ego or self resides. A balanced sacral chakra reflects in your wonderful sense of equanimity and a deep sense of security that does not have an iota of submissiveness. Invoking this chakra while envisioning your future will help create a beautiful image of what you want to achieve which, in turn, will empower you to work hard to achieve your dream(s).

The Solar Plexus or Navel Chakra – the Third Tier of Consciousness

As the toddler grows and begins to understand things around him, learns to speak and sing in the language used at home, and finds his ego, the next step in the evolution of the consciousness is stories. Look at your own life when you around 4 years and until you were around 10, perhaps, give or take a few years.

These years would be replete with stories told to you by your parents, grandparents, uncles, and aunts. Stories from your classmates would have been fascinating as well, isn't it? Stories are a big part of our growing up years and this is true of the evolution of our consciousness too.

Once the spoken language had evolved fairly well, man began to look at stories to grow up, learn, mature, and move up in the level of consciousness. As he listened to stories, he was able to discern the different roles played by different characters in the story and using these roles, he began to connect with one or more roles. He connected each role with the power and authority that the character wielded.

This third level of consciousness is the stage when an individual comes into his or her own. He or she realizes the power of the self and the ability in the individual's power to rewrite or change the course of the story.

The Navel Chakra that is open and well-balanced gives you the power to control and guide the reins of your own life. When this chakra is robust, you are charged up to drive and follow your dreams and ambitions.

As part of the human evolution, you can connect this stage of consciousness as one in which man learned to plow his own fields and sow seeds and reap the fruits of his own labor. This was the stage when man built weapons and used them to conquer and enhance his territories. This was the stage when everyone had a chosen role to play and that role had a fixed place in society.

There was a place for the farmer, for the trader, for the manufacturer, for the shipbuilder, for the king, for the adviser, etc. There was a designated place for the commoner, the king, and the priest. If you notice, the priest who appeased the furies of nature and worshipped gods and goddesses that is representative of the root chakra remains powerful now too.

An individual with a powerful third chakra or a robust third level of consciousness will find the power to break existing boundaries and charter his or her own territories because he believed in the power of his own story. With a powerful third chakra, you find the fire to break barriers, to follow through with your desires and dreams.

The Sanskrit name for the navel chakra is 'Manipura' which translates to 'jewel city.' 'Mani' is a jewel and 'pura' is a city. This is the center of your body and is the seat of fire. It represents a place of personal aura and power. In terms of consciousness, this 3rd level represents a stage wherein we recognize perceived and real authority and this knowledge empowers us to see through perceptions and value true authority.

This is also the stage in the evolution of our consciousness wherein we recognize our own power to break through limiting beliefs and barriers that are thwarting our growth trajectory. When the spiritual energy is awakened in this stage, it translates into an inner awakening that brings forth manifest changes in the way you lead your life.

Fire is the element represented by this chakra. The energy of the manipura chakra has a natural tendency to move upwards just like the flames in a fire. If you have clear ideas and intentions in your life, the fire of this chakra will help you forge ahead to achieve your dreams.

The basic quality of this stage of consciousness is 'transformation.' When you are aware of this chakra's powers and your own ability, you are transformed from being a victim to becoming victorious, from having a fatalistic attitude to having a creative bend of mind, and from depending on others to becoming the maker of your own destiny.

Methods of Balancing the Solar Plexus Chakra

Mantra – Chant 'ram' (rhyming with 'hum) seven times each day. While chanting, visualize a wheel of golden yellow light spinning at the position of the solar plexus chakra. This will help in releasing the energy and balancing the third chakra. Affirmations like 'I create my own destiny,' 'I don't follow anyone else's destiny,' 'I am my own master,' etc help in soothing the frayed nerves of self-confidence empowering you to find and forge your own life path.

Meditation – Meditating in front of a flame (from a lamp or a candle) is very effective to open this chakra. Gaze gently at the flame while visualizing a bright flame in your belly slowly gaining strength and power of its own.

Diet – Foods to awaken the solar plexus chakra include bananas and bread. Grains like rye, flax, and rice are effective too. Dairy products including milk, cheese, curd, etc are good to release energy from the solar plexus chakra. Spices that work well for this third chakra include fennel, chamomile, cumin, and mint.

The solar plexus or the Manipura chakra is the center of your being. It is the seat where the fire of your life burns. It represents self-assertiveness and reflects your ability to express yourself. A weak manipura chakra can result in a weak life that is being controlled by everyone else but you. A fired up manipura chakra is necessary to charge up your warrior energy to fight and win the struggles of life as you make your own destiny and live your own dreams.

CHAPTER 3B:

CHAKRAS AND THE EVOLUTION OF HUMAN CONSCIOUSNESS - PART 2

This is a continuation of the last chapter and we will discuss the remaining four chakras and their associations with our consciousness.

The Heart Chakra – the Fourth Tier of Consciousness

The heart is the most beautiful organ in our entire body not just because the working of the heart connects every nook and cranny of your body but also because this wonderful piece of art has the ability to connect the seen and the unseen, the tangible and the intangible, and the lover and the loved. It is an unending bridge allowing you to connect everything within and outside of you.

The beauty and power of the heart are felt only when you have achieved all the materialistic comforts of life and yet, find the longing in your heart still left unfulfilled. That is when you realize that your heart needs hardly any physical comfort to heal and only needs love and care.

The human consciousness continued to evolve and we urged

our solar plexus chakra to fight and achieve our dreams and built a wonderful identity for ourselves. Despite luxuries and other achievements that we managed to win, man still felt an emptiness that seemed impossible to fill.

Quite often, our advisers told us many things that made sense to our minds but our hearts refused to accept these thoughts. We started questioning our desire to achieve dreams, we questioned our inability to find happiness even in the midst of riches and wealth, and we began again to question our faith and our ability to believe in God.

During this stage in the evolution of the human consciousness, logic and rationality were respected, science slowly gained popularity and, again, the individual became more important than the society or the community. We started our inward journey and began to look for answers from within us instead of the external world.

An open heart chakra means you have also risen to the 4th level of consciousness wherein you begin to search for joy in intangible things. You begin to realize that life is not about making money. Life is more than that. A freewheeling heart chakra slows down the other chakras as you find yourself delving deeper and deeper into you to find answers because you are now sure that important answers do not lie outside of you.

You connect with everyone around you with love and compassion and your heart and mind are totally open to every new experience willing to learn and absorb. The Sanskrit word for the heart chakra is 'anahata' or unhurt/ unstruck.

At this level of consciousness, you are moving from the physical and materialistic identities to spiritual identities. You are moving from the joy of receiving and achieving to the joy of letting go and sacrificing. When your spiritual energy is released at this level, you are filled with compassion and love for everything around you. You show empathy, sympathy, kindness, and forgiveness towards one and all without any sense of discrimination.

This stage can be compared to the cocoon building stage of the butterfly's life where it is building a cocoon around itself to save it from the external hazards. Here, you are building a cocoon around yourself to stop greed and gluttony from taking over your life. You stop yourself from running after external pursuits and instead, find the time and inclination to look deep within yourself to find the true meaning of life.

The element associated with the heart chakra is air. Like air, you feel a sense of freedom and joy when the heart chakra is opened and its energy released. The heart chakra's basic quality is love and compassion for one and all. The sense that is heightened when your heart chakra is opened is the sense of touch and embrace. This heightened sense of touch enhances the compassion and love you feel.

Methods of Balancing the Heart Chakra

Mantra – The mantra that works to balance your heart chakra is 'yam' (rhyming with 'hum'). Repeat this mantra seven times a day as you imagine a wheel of green light spinning at the location of your heart chakra. Affirmations like 'I love the world,' 'I feel loved,' etc. can also help in balancing the anahata chakra.

Meditation – Metta (which translates to loving-kindness) is a great way to meditate to balance your heart chakra. Sit quietly with your eyes closed. As you inhale deeply, visualize your heart being filled with loving breath and repeat, 'May I be happy and well.' When you have practiced on yourself, include the picture of a loved one and repeat 'May you be happy and well.' Slowly but surely you will find the wherewithal to include the entire universe to fit into your lap of love and compassion.

Diet – Green leafy vegetables are great to restore balance in the heart chakra that is associated with the color green. Cabbage, spinach, broccoli, kale, etc are great foods for the heart chakra. Herbs like thyme, mint, and basil are wonderful for your heart too.

The heart chakra is totally about compassion and love. Love comes back in a multiplier effect when you give love unconditionally. The heart pushes you to forgive and forget and move on in life and this attitude is the basis of personal success. The more you hold on to pain, the less you will feel loved. Let go of other people's mistakes and soon you will be able to forgive yourself too.

The Throat Chakra – the Fifth Tier of Consciousness

The throat chakra is known to be your voice box or your ability to express your thoughts and beliefs clearly and fearlessly. From the time civilization has started, aligning your talks to the popular trends of the society you come from is taught to us. We are conditioned to express only those thoughts that are politically correct and our raised voiced against injustices are suppressed by the society.

However, today's highly open and transparent world is enjoying being in this fifth tier of consciousness wherein we are finding the courage and strength to question senseless dogmas and argue for just causes as we celebrate our differences and yet find value in the unity of humanity.

Communication is sort of peaking in the evolution of human consciousness and thanks to the internet and the myriad social media platforms everyone is having an opinion and wants to articulate those opinions. If you have to find an analogy of this level of consciousness in the butterfly's metamorphosis stage, then it would be that of the chrysalis phase wherein it is finding its colors and its voice to represent itself.

Human beings are also at that stage where we are finding our voices and our identities that connect us to other human beings who think like us. An open and well-balanced throat chakra is the voice of your soul and body. It allows you to be expressive and creative and gives you the power to overcome limiting conditions to break free of traditions and find your voice.

The Sanskrit name of this chakra is vishuddha which translates to purity or clarity. The evolution of your consciousness to this fifth level will lend clarity of thought and articulation to the wisdom that you have gained within. When the spiritual energy is awakened at this level, you will find the skills of self-expression, courage, and communication increase to considerable levels.

The element of this chakra is that which is reflective of sound energy. The basic quality of this chakra is self-expression and an open throat chakra empowers you to articulate your beliefs with honesty and integrity and without putting down anyone else's beliefs. The sense that is in a heightened state when this chakra is open is your sense of hearing. With a powerful and well-balanced throat chakra, you will be able to listen with focus and attention the words of wisdom spoken to you.

Unfortunately, an overactive throat chakra can make a highly opinionated and abusive personality talking beyond need and without any sense too, sometimes. With a weak throat chakra, your messages can come across as dishonest and unclear.

Methods for Balancing the Throat Chakra

Mantra – The mantra for this chakra is 'hum.' Repeat it in a meditative state seven times a day while visualizing a blue-colored wheel spinning at the location of the throat chakra. Affirmations like 'I live by and say my truth,' will also help in opening up the throat chakra.

Meditation – The best form of meditation for the throat chakra is through the chanting of your favorite mantra or affirmation. Sit comfortably, close your eyes, and repeat your mantra over and over again in your head or as a whisper.

Diet – Herbal teas, liquids and fruit juices are great to soothe your throat. Lemongrass and lemon verbena are great for your throat. Citrus fruits like lemon, oranges, and kiwis are good too.

The throat chakra or the Vishuddha chakra is essential to find your voice and express your true feelings and beliefs without feeling constricted. When you are struggling to embrace and expressing your beliefs openly, opening up and releasing energy from the throat chakra will help you.

The Third Eye Chakra – the Sixth Tier of Consciousness

This extremely important chakra is one that goes beyond the five known and accepted sense of human beings. The third eye chakra has the power to see and feel elements that are beyond those of the average human being. With a well-aligned third eye chakra, you will be able to see the oneness and connectedness of the entire universe. You will be able to see and feel the harmony by connecting with the seen and the unseen aspects of our ever-expanding universe.

The human consciousness in its entirety has yet achieved this 6th level of consciousness. Yet, there have been, are, and will continue to be people who have been able to break the barriers of the five senses and reach this sixth tier of consciousness. When the third eye chakra is perfectly balanced, you will automatically get the gift of intuition and the power to perceive the universe as one and completely connected.

The third eye chakra views the world as an objective observer and when you achieve this near-impossible task, you can proudly call yourself as being on the same level as the yogis and the saints. When the third eye is activated, it is believed that the right and the left hemispheres of your brain look at things in a unifying way without discrimination and without subjectivity.

The Sanskrit name of the third eye chakra is 'Ajna' or command. This is the command center of your entire being. This is the seat of wisdom wherein your consciousness evolves into something so powerful that you are able to see, access, and experience life from a much deeper place of insight and wisdom that cannot be explained but can only be experienced. When spiritual energy is awakened in this state, you gain access to intuition and inner guidance.

The element connected to the Ajna chakra is the mind which is also believed to be made up of the same five senses that our earthly bodies are made of. This chakra can even transcend the five elements of the mind opening your system to a universal intelligence. The basic quality of this chakra is insight, wisdom, and intuition. The sixth sense is in a heightened state when the Ajna chakra is activated.

An overactive third eye chakra can result in headaches and sometimes, you could get delusional too. An underactive third eye chakra, on the other hand, reflects a lack of spiritual understanding. For the ordinary people, a third eye chakra that is working at a less-than-average efficiency could result in situations where you cannot take clear and sound decisions. You cannot judge wisely and objectively and there is a general feeling of confusion in your mind.

Methods for Balancing the Third Eye Chakra

Mantra – The mantra recommended by the yogis to activate the third eye chakra is 'Aum' (rhyming with 'home'). Inhale deeply, first. Then, as you exhale, start the sound of 'Aaaaaa' from your belly, then gradually convert it to the 'uuuuu' and finally, end with a humming 'mmmm.' Repeat this every day 9 or 11 times. When you have achieved perfection in the method of saying the mantra, you can repeat it 21 times every day.

Meditation – Sit comfortably and close your eyes. Keep your thoughts focused on an indigo-colored wheel spinning in your forehead between your eyes. Focus as long as you can. If you are getting a headache or feeling uncomfortable, then stop and you can continue later on.

Diet – Blue-colored fruits and vegetables such as eggplants, blueberries, juniper, etc. are good for activating the third eye chakra. The herbs that are conducive to activating the ajna chakra include rosemary, lavender, and sage. Foods rich in Omega-3 fatty acids like flax seeds and walnuts are great as well.

An open, clear, and balanced third eye chakra is essential for you to discover the purpose of your life. Moreover, an active and well-balanced third eye chakra will help you tap into the limitless energies of the universe.

The Crown Chakra – the Seventh Tier of Consciousness

This is the ultimate level of consciousness wherein all the wisdom and knowledge gained during our present and past lifetimes converge into pure wisdom. Until such time, you are able to achieve the seventh level of consciousness, you are actually living a life of belief. Only when you have reached this level and activated the crown chakra will you be living a life of experience.

There is a difference between gaining knowledge and achieving wisdom. Gaining knowledge has to do with collecting data and trying to analyze it with our minds. Wisdom is converting that data into an experiential thing and living life by it. The opening of the Crown Chakra will release you from the deception of duality and let you experience the oneness of this entire universe. Until now, you would have only believed in the Supreme Power or God! At this stage of consciousness, you become one with that Supreme Power or God!

Again, as a species, the human race has not yet evolved into this high level of consciousness. Yet, there have been souls in the past and in the present (rarely do they walk amongst the public) who have been able to reach this level. They help mankind by simply being here.

At this stage, there is nothing left to do or to prove. You are complete and total. Again, this level cannot be explained but only experienced. Sages and saints who have been able to tap the universal energy at this level of consciousness don't feel any disconnect with anything or anyone in this universe. They are able to see the unity in all beings.

The Sanskrit name of the Crown Chakra is 'Sahasrara' which means a 'lotus with thousand petals.' This is the last stage of the evolution of human consciousness. It opens the door to Pure Consciousness. When you achieve this status, you will not need to read this book any more. You've gone beyond the realm of human beings.

The element associated with the Crown Chakra is Energy that is nothing but pure consciousness and pure awareness. The basic quality of this chakra is eternal bliss where no pain exists; perhaps, the Utopian world as some would like to put it. As you are connected with everyone and everything around you, the sense that is most heightened when the Crown Chakra is activated is empathy.

A weak Crown Chakra is reflective of a person who is not interested in following and understanding the spiritual path. It is unlikely that such people will ever experience spiritual experiences. An overactive Crown Chakra, on the other hand, makes you want to play God! It is better to have a weak Crown Chakra than an overactive one, believe me!

Methods of Balancing the Crown Chakra

Mantra – There is no mantra except silence to activate this crown chakra. Yet, the sound of 'Om' could help with starting off. Sit comfortably and use your thumbs to close your ears. Then repeat 'Om' 21 times. Now, place your hands on your knees and slowly repeat 'Om' again until you taper off into silence.

Meditation – Sitting comfortably with your eyes closed, imagine a thousand-petal lotus at the top of your head. Imagine each of the petals opening one by one with the white light that is emanating from it pervading your entire body. Feel yourself connecting with the universe as a whole as your body seems to simply merge into nothingness.

Diet – Unprocessed and raw foods along with plenty of water are the best combination to activate the Crown Chakra. This is as close as you can get to nature without starving yourself.

An open Crown Chakra matches your frequency with that of the Universe resulting in perfect resonance and unison leaving you feeling completely connected with the cosmos and all things in it.

Remember your body is merely the gross manifestation of a powerful form of energy that makes up this entire Universe. As you move slowly but steadily up the seven levels of consciousness, you will find yourself being freed from different bonds and attachments at each level. At the final level of consciousness, you are nothing but pure awareness experiencing nothing but eternal bliss.

CHAPTER 4:

THE BENEFIT OF THE DIFFERENT CHAKRAS

The chakras are important for so many different parts of your body. They are going to help you to feel good when they are all in alignment. But when the chakras stop working the way that they should, you will find that it can be frustrating. When one chakra gets out of line, it isn't going to take too much longer before all of the chakras start to fail as well. You need to have all of the chakras lined up properly to ensure that you are getting all the benefits that you are looking for. Before you can work on increasing how well your chakras work, you need to know more about how all of the chakras work and why you would want to help them to get better. Here are some of the benefits that you can get when it comes to working with your chakras.

The Root Chakra

The first chakra to look at is the root chakra. This chakra is in charge of your foundation and can help you to feel grounded in reality. You will be able to find this chakra near the base of the spine, kind of near the tailbone area. When the root chakra is working properly, you will be able to feel grounded in reality and will feel pretty secure. But some of the emotional issues that are associated with the root chakra include survival issues like food, money and even financial independence.

Balancing the root or the base chakra will help the negative emotions in your body to become released. This helps you to gain more of the confidence that you are looking for and will encourage you to move forward with your life. A healthy root or base chakra can promote feelings of security and will help you to explore around in order to find your purpose and to achieve success. A root chakra that is balanced is also able to generate the flow of energy all over to the other chakras.

The Sacral Chakra

The sacral chakra is the one that is responsible for your connection and how well you are able to accept people who are different from you in your life. If you are having trouble trying out new things or meeting new people, there could be an issue with your sacral chakra. This one is going to be found in your lower abdomen and it is near the navel and a little bit in. The emotional issues that are associated with the sacral chakra include having abundance, pleasure and how good you feel.

Balancing out the sacral chakra will help you to feel more confidence and energy in all of the aspects of your life. You will feel really inspired and your life will just seem to flow. People will be attracted to some of your positive energy and many opportunities are going to start opening up for you. With a sacral chakra that is open, you will be able to live right now in the moment and to experience life to the fullest. You will also see that your stamina will increase, so many physical tasks will become easier.

The Solar Plexus Chakra

The solar plexus chakra is all about your confidence levels. If you feel that someone else is in charge of your life or you aren't able to make decisions for yourself, there could be an issue with the solar plexus chakra not working the right way. You will be able to find the solar plexus chakra in the upper stomach area. The emotional issues that are found in the solar plexus chakra will include self-esteem, self-confidence, and self-worth. When these are not working properly, it is hard to have the right amount of confidence to get things done during the day!

Being able to balance out the solar plexus chakra will allow you to feel a bit more centered in your spirit, body, and mind. You will be comfortable in your own skin and will be able to relax a bit more. The energy that comes from this chakra is going to permeate to some of the other chakras, which helps you to relieve some of the other psychological and physical disorders that are going on in your body. It will also allow you to become a bit more aware of your own energy and how to be more comfortable with your own decisions, such as following your intuition or your gut feelings.

The Heart Charka

The heart chakra is the one that is in charge of your ability to love. It is in charge of your feelings and how well you can feel compassion or not to others. If this one works well, you have the right emotions and love for the people in your life. When it is closed or blocked you may not feel love or concern for anyone and when it is too open, you feel emotions all of the time because they go overboard so much. You will be able to find the heart chakra right at the center of the chest, just a little bit above the heart. The emotional issues that are associated with the heart chakra include love, inner peace, and joy.

Balancing the heart chakra will help you to enhance your love for others as well as the love you feel for yourself. It allows you to have feelings of forgiveness, empathy, and compassion for the world around you. When this chakra is in good working order, you are able to connect with a world vision of the beauty around you just like a child would. With this chakra, harmony and peace are going to flourish in your relationships with yourself and with others.

The Throat Chakra

The throat chakra is the one that is in charge of your ability to communicate. When it is working properly, you know when the perfect circumstances are to speak up and talk to others. You can have good communication with others without being shy or talk too much. You will be able to find the throat chakra right at the throat. The emotional issues that are associated with the throat chakra include communication, self-expression of feelings and the truth when speaking to others.

Balancing out the throat chakra means that you are able to have more open communication and you don't have as many issues with expressing your feelings. You are also able to do these things without feeling judgment from others. It is going to promote more harmony and honesty with your actions and your feelings because you are able to live a life that is more free and authentic.

A throat chakra that is balanced is going to help you to be more successful with your communication inside of relationships and even at work. It can be really important if you are in a career that relies on self-expression and communication so working on this chakra can be very important in some circumstances.

The Third Eye Chakra

The third eye chakra is all about your ability to focus on and see the big picture of what is going on around you. When the third eye chakra is not working properly, it is hard to see the other side of arguments or of the story and you may become too focused on a little piece, holding onto it for dear life and getting into bad fights because you refuse to expand your thinking and look at the full picture. You will be able to find this chakra right on the forehead between the eyes and sometimes it is called the Brow Chakra. The emotional issues that are associated with this one include intuition, imagination, wisdom, and the ability to think and make decisions when it matters most.

Balancing the third eye chakra is going to help you to promote innovation, inspiration, and clarity. It is going to allow you to better follow your dreams and will enhance your innate spiritual connections and your psychic abilities. When the third eye chakra is balanced, it can help you to process out the timeline of your own lives, which means that you are able to learn from what you did in the past, how to be present right now, and then how to see the best way to reach success in the future.

When the third eye chakra is balanced well, you will find that your intuition is much stronger and even clearer and dream interpretation is fairly easy. You will also be able to form a deep connection with the universal plan of your life. When the third eye chakra is able to guide you through your universal plan, you will have a sense of more doors and possibilities opening up to you to help you reach your goals.

The Crown Chakra

The crown chakra is the highest chakra in the body and it is in charge of representing your ability to be fully connected spiritually. It is located at the top of the head and it is responsible for helping you to feel happy and connected with the universe around you, or with whatever spiritual realm you focus on. The emotional issues that come with the crown chakra include your inner and outer beauty, your connection to your own spirituality and pure bliss.

All of these chakras come together to help you live a life that is full and complete. When all of the chakras are in good working order, you will feel complete and whole. You will be able to understand other points of view, you will feel happy, and you will be able to love others around you. But when one of the chakras gets blocked or opened up too wide, it is going to start to affect the others, especially if you don't take the time to get it fixed as quickly as possible. This guidebook will spend some time talking about some of the things that you can do to help heal the chakras so they are all in good working order.

Balancing the crown chakra is really important if you would like to have a spiritual and deep connection within yourself, with God, and with the universe. The energy that is able to enter and then leave this chakra will help to facilitate your flow of positive energy through the other six chakras. It is also responsible for helping to create the outlook that you have in life.

Benefits of Keeping Your Chakras Aligned

It is important to keep your chakras as balanced as possible for your good health. Your chakras are able to influence everything that you do and there are many things that can make them get unbalanced. From the little stresses that go on in your life to the illnesses that you may be dealing with, it is not uncommon to find that your chakras are not as aligned as they should be.

In this modern world, it is especially hard to keep those chakras going nice and strong. You want to make sure that they are providing the best benefit for yourself so that you can feel happy, show love to others and get the most out of life, but there is just so much that can happen to those chakras that will make you feel sick or angry or just have trouble getting through the day.

If you want to make sure that you are getting through the stress that comes with your modern day life and you want to ensure that you are able to stay happy and healthy, then it is really important that you learn how to align your chakras. There are many ways that you are able to balance those chakras and help you to live a holistic life, you just need to choose the one that works the best for your needs.

When you are able to finally align those chakras, you are going to see such a huge difference in your quality of life. You won't have to worry about feeling sick as often, or about being stressed out and anxious about all the little things in your life. You will be able to connect with other people and feel welcome wherever you go and you can make smart decisions that are beneficial to you and those around you. While too many people ignore their chakras and what they all entail, these chakras can be really important to your overall health and will help you to improve so many aspects of your personal life.

CHAPTER 5:

AWAKENING YOUR SEVEN CHAKRAS

Now, it's time to start awakening your chakras.

It is important that you awaken your chakras before you use them for your own healing. All people have chakras in their body; these points aren't just active. A re-birthing session must take place first before you awaken your chakras. During the re-birthing stage, you have to exhale in a relaxed way. Visualize that the air you breathe is passing through your chakra points.

1. Root Chakra:

To awaken your root chakra, first, stand with your feet wide apart. Make sure that you are comfortable. Next, rotate your hips from right to left. Do this about 48 to 50 times. Breathe deeply as you rotate your hips, and take three directed breaths when you're done. Repeat the same procedure (hip rotation) from left to right. Follow this with three directed breaths.

2 & 3. Navel Center Chakra:

Just like in the root chakra, take 49 to 50 re-birthing breaths and then tuck your stomach in sharply. You don't want to harm yourself when you get started with this one, but do draw your stomach back a little bit to help you to work on the navel center chakra. This will make a big difference in how much you will be able to feel this particular chakra.

4. Heart Chakra:

Awaken your heart chakra by stretching your arms sideways. Take 49 re-breathing breaths whole moving your arms in a circular manner. Move your arms up and down, and then take three directed breaths. Repeat the process.

5. Throat Chakra:

Drop your head forward and then do a head roll, first to the left, then to the back, and then forward. As you move your head, breathe deeply. You must be able to have 7 re-birthing breaths after each head roll.

6. Third Eye:

Empower your third eye by taking 49 re-birthing breaths and raising your eyebrows quickly as you open your eyes. After that, close your eyes and concentrate on your breathing.

7. Crown Chakra:

Raise your arms as you take seven directed breaths. Feel the energy and imagine it encircling you from head to foot.

Balancing Your Chakras

Balancing your seven chakras is important because when one of your chakras is not balanced, your emotions and your body might be affected. When you are with someone who is sad or happy, it is highly possible for you to channel these emotions.

You become a magnet of energy! However, too much bad energy could weaken your state, and you could feel ill. Be responsible for your own emotions. The information below will guide you as to what happens when there is an imbalance in your emotions:

Anger gives you flashes of red. This is such a strong energy that emanates from a person – too much of it is bad for your body as it absorbs other negative elements. When you are angry, know that there is a chakra imbalance in the solar plexus. You also see flashes of red; perhaps this is where the expression "seeing red" came from.

On the other hand, being defensive puts armors or cords around you. Defensiveness signals an imbalance in your brow and solar plexus chakras. Whenever this happens, you feel that you want to alienate yourself from other people. You dislike relationships and reject pieces of advice and help from friends and relatives.

Resentment clouds your vision. Almost similar to anger, resentment makes you unable to think clearly. Making decisions is also difficult for you. There is definitely an imbalance in the heart and solar plexus. The same thing happens when you are really sad. It's like there is a cloud before your eyes. This means there is an imbalance in your heart and crown chakras. Address this quickly. Otherwise, you could feel depressed and anxious.

Jealousy, in contrast, enables hooks of energy to trap you. You feel angry and resentful at the same time. You want to pour your energy into things that aren't worth your time – being jealous. You also become possessive of people. Remember that there is an imbalance of the heart, solar plexus and brow plexus. Lastly, hysteria results in fragmentation. You feel disconnected. There will be times when you can't explain and express what you feel. Communication is difficult. Hysteria is the worst form of emotional and auric disturbance; hence, all the chakras are affected.

Bringing Back the Balance to Your Chakras

To rebalance your chakras, first, you have to create a sacred space for yourself. You could use natural elements here; either surround yourself with the elements that represent fire, water, wind, and earth; or you use your crystals and gemstones to create a sacred circle. Sprinkle salt around the sacred circle to purify it. Next, ground yourself and connect with the energy of the earth. A simple way to do this is to lie on the floor.

Connect with the cosmic energy as well. Imagine that there is a golden energy or a yellow light surrounding you. This light comes from your crown chakra, passes to your heart chakra region, then to your hands. Imagine this light going down to your toes.

Say an affirmation or a prayer to invite your spirit guide, or to at least welcome the cosmic energy. You could start with the "I Have the Right" affirmation. Since the chakras are connected to your body and your emotions, you can say this prayer and mantra. Breathe deeply and concentrate as you say these statements:

I have the right to basic needs.
I feel that my basic needs will be fulfilled soon.
I have the right to feel safe and valued.
I have the right to feel nurtured.
I have the right to address my desires.
I have the right to make decisions for myself.
I have the right to say no to things I don't want to do.

I have the right to love freely.
I have the right to be loved.
I have the right to feel that I am loved.
I have the right to communicate the truth.
I have the right to enjoy the world.
I have the right to fulfill my dreams.
I have the right to learn what the Higher Being teaches.

The next step is to scan the aura thrice. Do this with your dominant hand, as you lie on your back. Start at the top of the head, then use your hand to go over your body down to your feet. Be sensitive to where your chakras are blocked. If you feel any difficulty, use your pendulum to do that for you.

Note on pendulums: Any necklace will do, actually, but it is best to use a crystal dangling from a necklace. Use your intuition when choosing a pendulum.

Open your chakras using your dominant hand. Imagine a golden light coming from your hand and use it to go over your body. Spin your dominant hand 3 times to scan your aura. This will get rid of your blockages. Lastly, the pendulum will guide you to where your energies are blocked. As you hold the pendulum upright, say "I am now testing the ___ chakra. Is this blocked?" Make sure that you have assigned certain movements as responses (i.e. swinging back and forth as "yes" and rotating counterclockwise as "no".

When the pendulum says that, there are areas that are blocked, use your hand to balance the chakra point. Move your hand on top of the blocked region and imagine the golden light from your hands cleansing the area blockage. After moving your hand across the blocked chakra point, refer to your pendulum to check if the blockage has been removed.

If the chakra point has been opened, seal the positive energy by spinning the golden light from your hands on that chakra point three times, counterclockwise. Sweep your hand from the top of your head down to your feet to seal the auras. When you are done, cross your arms over your chest and thank your spirit guides.

CHAPTER 6:

CHAKRAS, ENDOCRINE SYSTEM AND THE IMMUNE SYSTEM

The last few chapters spoke about the different chakras, their locations, and benefits. In addition to the benefits mentioned earlier, there are many things that chakras control including the efficient functioning of our endocrine system and our emotions. Let us look at each in a bit of detail:

Let us start by recalling the 7 primary chakras and their locations:

1. Root Chakra – situated at the base of the spine
2. Sacral Chakra – situated below the navel
3. Solar Plexus Chakra – situated above the navel
4. Heart Chakra – situated in the middle of the chest
5. Throat Chakra – situated in the throat
6. Third Eye Chakra – situated at the center of the forehead
7. Crown Chakra – situated at the top of the head

The Endocrine System

Next, let us look at the Endocrine System in our body. The Endocrine System is our body's central mechanism of control. It consists of many ductless glands that are responsible for secreting, producing, and distributing different kinds of hormones required for various physiological functions of our body.

These hormones are directly sent through the bloodstream to the places that need them. Effective functioning of the Endocrine System is essential for overall good physical and mental health. The Endocrine System consists of the following elements:

The Pineal Gland – The most important hormone secreted by this gland is melatonin that is responsible for maintaining and regulating your body's circadian rhythm or the internal biological clock. This cone-shaped gland along with the pituitary gland regulates and balances the entire biological and glandular functioning in our body. The third eye chakra can be activated optimally when the pineal and the pituitary glands work perfectly in tandem.

The Pituitary Gland – Also referred to as the 'master gland,' the pituitary gland controls the activities and functioning of most other glands. Attached to the hypothalamus (between the eyes), the pituitary gland regulates the functioning of other organs and other glands. It communicates via signals in different forms.

This pea-shaped gland works in tandem with the pineal gland controls and balances the overall smooth functioning of our body's physiological and biological activities. The energy of the third eye chakra can be released when these two glands are well synchronized with each other.

Pancreas – The two kinds of hormones produced by the pancreas are needed for two basic functions; one to aid in digestion and the other to control energy levels in our body.

Ovaries – These glands produce the female hormones namely progesterone and estrogen and also produce and release eggs for reproduction

Testes – These glands come in pairs and are responsible for the production and release of the male hormone, testosterone. They also produce and release sperms.

Thyroid – A very important gland, the thyroid is responsible for regulating the heart rate, the metabolic rate and also controls a few digestive functions along with bone maintenance, muscle control, and brain development. The thyroxin produced by the thyroid controls the rate at which our body converts stored food into energy for use. A malfunctioning thyroid can be quite a debilitating factor that comes in the way of a leading a happy life for anyone.

Parathyroid – This gland controls calcium levels in the bloodstream so that the muscles and the nerves function smoothly. The parathyroid also helps in keeping bones healthy and strong.

Hypothalamus – This gland responds to multiple external and internal factors and triggers various reactions to enable stability and a consistent state in our body. The hypothalamus triggers various physiological reactions in response to feelings of hunger, the temperature of your body, feelings of excessive eating, blood pressure, and others. Based on these conditions, it sends signals to other glands and organs to respond appropriately to these triggers to enable a stable and consistent condition of your body.

Adrenal Glands – These glands secrete different kinds of hormones referred to as 'chemical messengers' which travel through the bloodstream to triggers physiological and chemical reactions in various organs.

The Immune System

Millions and millions of cells come together and waltz together in perfect harmony exchanging critical information thereby triggering appropriate and important physiological, biological, and chemical reactions in our body. The cells of the immune system help organs and organ systems in our body to function smoothly helping us live a happy and peaceful life.

Moreover, those cells that are not performing optimally are retired and new ones are automatically generated to take their place thereby enhancing our health and our longevity. If these weak cells are not correctly replaced in the immune system, they end up sending erroneous signals to all parts of the body resulting in disorders and discomforts such as weak digestion, general body weakness and delayed recovery from even simple illnesses.

The way modern medicines work to set this right is by suppressing the action of the well-functioning cells too until such time all the cells do not achieve the same level of functioning. The medication is continued until all the cells in the immune system get back into the synchronized dancing pattern. This is where chakra healing can help in getting our immune system in order.

The Thymus Gland – It is an important gland to be included in this chapter because of it is very closely related to the immune system. It plays an important role in the production of T-cells which form an essential part of the white blood cells that form the core of our immune system. In fact, if you speak to any chakra healer, he or she will tell you the dance of the immune system is the most beautiful and well-coordinated dance in our body.

Chakras and Glands

If you notice the locations of the glands, you will see that they are more or less placed close to different chakras. Although the traditional systems do not speak about the connection between chakras and glands, the modern followers and experts started outlining clear connections between the various chakras, glands, organs and the immune system of the body.

Each chakra is connected to different glands of the endocrine system and facilitates the smooth functioning of that particular gland. Here is a list of the various chakras, the glands they regulate, their functions and the signs of warnings associated with an inefficiently functioning gland/chakra:

Root Chakra – This is connected to the adrenal glands and stands for self-preservation and physical energy. The issues that the root chakra and the adrenal glands handle are associated with survival and security. In the males, the sacral chakra is closely linked to the gonads. The fight/flight response of the adrenal glands located at the top of the kidneys is directly connected to the survival drive of the root chakra.

A weak root chakra could result in a weakened metabolism and immune system resulting from a compromised working of the adrenal glands which are responsible for releasing and producing chemical messengers needed for all the physiological, chemical and biological functions of your body.

A not-so-strong root chakra results in nervousness and a sense of insecurity whereas an overly working root chakra could result in greed and a sense of excessive materialism.

Sacral Chakra – Governs the reproductive glands which are the ovaries (for the females) and the testes (for the males. The well-balanced and healthy root chakra facilitates the uninterrupted functioning of these glands ensuring well-developed sexuality in the person.

The root chakra also regulates the production and secretion of the sex hormones. The potential for life formation in the ovaries is reflected in the sacral chakra as these two energies are connected.

When this chakra is open and free, you are able to express your sexuality well without being overly emotional. You feel a comforting sense of intimacy with your partner. A healthy sacral chakra enhances your passion and liveliness and helps you manage your sexuality without feeling burdened with undue emotions.

A sacral chakra that is not functioning at its peak efficiency is bound to leave you frigid, very close to people and relationships, and poker-faced. On the contrary, a weak sacral chakra will make you feel overly and unnecessarily, emotionally compelling you to attach yourself to people for a sense of security and belonging. Your feelings could be overly sexual towards one and all.

Solar Plexus Chakra – This controls the pancreas, which is directly connected to the sugar (through the control of insulin secretion) and, therefore, energy levels in your body. Thus, if this chakra is not working properly you could potentially have a weak pancreas, resulting in a compromised metabolic state. Compromised pancreas could lead to digestive problems, lowered blood sugar levels, ulcers, poor memory, etc. which are all connected with a bad metabolism.

Heart Chakra – Regulates the thymus gland and through it, the entire immune system. Being the center of love, compassion, spirituality, and group consciousness, a malfunctioning heart chakra will result in the malfunctioning of the thymus gland leaving you prone to low immunity.

Our feelings and thoughts towards ourselves play a crucial role in keeping our immune system working well. When we love ourselves our immune system is powerful and strong. When we are uncertain of ourselves and our strengths and our capabilities, we feel disappointed which drives us to react wrongly to negative things.

All these negativities leave our immune system weak and we end up holding on to toxins. It is imperative to keep our heart chakra healthy by investing time and energy in self-love so that our immune system is strengthened. An underactive heart chakra makes you feel distant and cold and an overactive one could result in selfish love in your heart. Be wary of both states and work at keeping your chakra balanced.

Throat Chakra – controls and regulates the thyroid gland and hence is directly responsible for a healthy metabolism and to regulate body temperature. This is the center of communication and plays a vital role in the way you speak, write, or think. An unbalanced throat chakra results in a malfunctioning thyroid resulting in an overall poor physical, mental, and emotional health.

Third Eye Chakra – directly controls the functioning of the pituitary gland or the master gland which controls and regulates other organs and glands in the human body. The Pineal gland is many times associated with this chakra too, as we already know that a well-coordinated, combined working of the pineal and the pituitary glands is responsible to keep our entire body, mind, and spirit well-oiled and working well.

Crown Chakra – This regulates the functioning of the pineal gland, which controls our biological cycle and our circadian rhythm.

Connection between Glands and Chakras

Even the slightest disturbances in the chakras or our energy centers can result in physical manifestations of issues and problems. When the chakras don't function efficiently the corresponding glands and organs they are associated with are also affected.

Chakras as you already know are the energy centers in our body and have no physiological or physical shape or form. These energy centers influence the way we live in different layers of our lives, including the biological, the physical, the emotional, and the psychic layers.

When any of the energy centers malfunction or become imbalanced, the problems are manifested in a physical, mental, or spiritual form. An underactive or an overactive chakra can cause problems for you. Keeping them balanced is critical for your overall health.

Any disturbance even in one energy center could result in problems in any other chakra and/or related glands and organs. For example, if there is a blockage in the heart chakra, you are going to feel unloved or listless or could have high blood pressure etc. All these problems could affect other organs which, in turn, can potentially harm associated chakras.

Therefore, it is imperative to keep all chakras in perfect balance to achieve overall physical, emotional, and spiritual health for yourself. Let us look at some examples of how a malfunctioning of chakras can affect the associated gland.

The Third Eye Chakra and the Pituitary and the Pineal Glands

When the third eye chakra is imbalanced or not working at its peak of efficiency, the functioning of both the pineal and pituitary glands will be affected leading to associated problems. For example, the pituitary is the master gland that regulates the functioning of other glands. So, when the third eye chakra is inefficient, other glands can also be affected negatively resulting in an overall breakdown of your systems.

The pituitary gland regulates intellect and emotion and working in conjunction with the pineal gland helps achieve overall balance in your body. The pineal gland will either resonate or counter the effects of pituitary gland for optimum benefit to our body and mind. Therefore, the third eye chakra is required to be given a lot of importance during your chakra healing and maintenance process.

The Heart Chakra and the Thymus Gland

Located in the middle of your chest, the heart chakra or the anahata controls and regulates the working of the thymus gland which is an important aspect of our immune system. A calm and balanced heart chakra results in an effectively-working nervous system and prevents undue agitation of your mind.

Here is a simple technique to help connect and activate your thymus gland. Tap gently in the middle of your chest at the collarbone level with your fingers. This helps in calming down agitated nerves. When you gently tap at the collar level about 3-4 inches away on each side helps to increase your energy levels.

Glands and Chakra Healing

Chakra healing will lead to improved functioning of the endocrine system which is great for physical healing of your body. The connection between glands and chakras represent a link between the energy points in your body to the physiological and physical functions.

Another useful entry point for chakra healing is the nervous system which is connected to glands and organs in multiple ways and at multiple points. A chakra healing session is ideally begun by calming the nerves and then targeting a particular gland and/or chakra.

By understanding the connection between chakras and the glands, you can use healing in different ways that will help you overcome physical, emotional, mental, and spiritual issues in your body and mind. Connecting the chakras and the glands will help in your overall well-being.

CHAPTER 7:

CHAKRAS AND PLANETS

It is unfortunate that we have lost our ability to imagine and use symbolism the way our ancient sages and saints used them to understand and notate their learning from the elements of this vast universe. As civilization progressed, our materialistic pursuits seemed to have overtaken our spiritual pursuits and the deep meanings of rituals and rites have been lost in translation and have sadly been reduced to seemingly meaningless rituals.

Today's students are taught concepts of outer space as astronomy leaving little or no connection to how the planets and other heavenly bodies affect our inner self. For most modern-day students and people, it is almost impossible to connect the effects of heavenly bodies especially planets in our daily lives.

The ancient explorers first explored their inner selves and then found connections in their external world. These connections did exist. All spiritual traditions are connected to first learning and understanding your inner self. Spiritual traditions evolved into modern-day medicine, astronomy, crystal healing, etc.

The seven primary chakras in our body are deeply connected to the various planets and other heavenly bodies in our universe. As the ancient sages learned and understood these chakras or energy centers in their bodies, they were able to find connections with heavenly bodies such as planets as well.

These wise men found that as planets moved or changed direction depending on their natural orbits, conflicts and/or alignments took place within their bodies. These were manifest in activities and creativities that were either enhanced or suppressed depending on the movement and positioning of each planet in relation to the chakras in the human body. Here are some connections with planets and the chakras:

The Crown Chakra – the seventh level of consciousness – is related to the planet Uranus. The expression associated with this chakra is 'I understand' and reflects expansion, openness, and generosity.

The Third Eye Chakra – the sixth level of consciousness – related to the planet Neptune and its expression is 'I see.' It controls limitations, time, and inevitable consequences of our past and present karmas.

The Throat Chakra – the fifth level of consciousness – is related to the planet Mercury and Jupiter and its expression is 'I speak.' It reflects creativity and communication.

The Heart Chakra – the fourth level of consciousness – is related to the planet Venus and its expression is 'I love.' This planet reflects compassion and peacefulness and happiness.

The Solar Plexus Chakra – the third level of consciousness – is related to the planet Sun and Mars and its expression is 'I do.'

It denotes brightness, optimism, and confidence.

The Sacral Chakra – the second level of consciousness – is related to the planet Pluto and its expression is 'I feel.' It represents spontaneity, sensuality, and tenderness.

The Root Chakra – the first level of consciousness – is related to the planet Saturn and its expression is 'I am.' It denotes stability and the ability to survive.

Planetary Interactions with Chakras

Now that there is a distinct connection between planets and the seven chakras, it is possible to leverage the power and influence of these planets to alter some aspects of our personality for increased happiness and success. Before we learn to do that, here is a word of caution. Any form of energy is powerful and that of a huge planet (no matter how far away it is from us) should never be underestimated. It is important that you know, accept, and respect the power of these planets.

Our past karmas decide the place and position of our birth along with how the planets will be placed when we come into this world again. All planets are sending both malefic and beneficial rays to the earth and it is up to our chakras how and what amount of these rays is received by our worldly body.

Some past karma could result in a malfunctioning of the root chakra in this birth and therefore, even when Saturn is sending beneficial rays, your blocked root chakra may not be in a position to accept and absorb these benefits. Therefore, it is essential that you clear and open up all the chakras in your system so that it is in the most conducive state to accept good rays and discard bad rays from the corresponding ruling planets.

The Root Chakra Ruled by Planet Saturn – Saturn is reflective of structure and your skeletal system is the basic structure that holds your entire body together. The skeletal system acts as a foundation or root. Bones, security, structure, and foundations are all connected with the first or the root chakra.

A weak root chakra means it is not clearly connected to the structure of the outside social world. Without strengthening your root chakra and without grounding yourself to the earth, you will simply survive from paycheck to paycheck in this highly competitive world where everyone is focusing on winning the 'rat race.'

Anxiety will be your middle name if your root chakra is not strong and there is a lack of power that can come from the powerful Saturn. If you are constantly worried about safety and security, you need to take a look at your surroundings.

Are you safe there? What are the causes of fear and insecurity? Can you find alternatives? When you awaken your first chakra, you will be compelled to take some tough and even unpopular decisions. Handle fear with equanimity and do not hesitate to stick to your tough decisions especially if you know it is good for you and your loved ones.

The Sacral Chakra Ruled by Pluto – Pluto represents the ability to change and transform driven by a desire for more than the basic physical needs of security and grounding offered by Saturn. With desire comes the ability to be creative. This is the place where your sensual and materialistic desires can be met and satisfied.

The problem with getting stuck with the changing and transforming the power of Pluto is that you run the risk of getting 'addicted' to sensual desires through physical means such as drugs, sex, etc. Yet, it is important to activate this chakra and call on the powers of Pluto to meet desires so that you can lead a happy and fulfilled life. It is important to remember when you are crossing the line of danger between getting your desires fulfilled in a meaningful way and the abysmal dangers of falling prey to addictions.

Love and sexual happiness with your committed partner are things to help you with realizing the power of this chakra. However, it is also possible to find pleasures in less lusty things like a simple hobby or art form that you can develop.

The Solar Plexus Chakra Ruled by Sun and Mars – This is the seat of sovereign power and represents your ability to build and maintain your own sense of identity without being coerced or compelled by others. The planet Mars is reflective of the warrior within you to fight your way from dogmas and limiting belief that threaten to smother your true and original identity.

The Sun radiates its light and either blinds us with its ferocity (the negative extreme of the spectrum) or helps us see and value our inner essence by lighting it up. People with a block solar plexus chakra are usually those who lack both warrior courage and the power of the sun to see their original selves and fight for a place on this earth for themselves. The Sun and the Mars in consonance help us see our inner radiance and achieve our dreams and desires.

These three chakras represent the physical aspects of our lives. It is imperative that we balance these three chakras and then only move on to the higher realms of consciousness including emotions which are beyond our physical body and senses.

The Heart Chakra Ruled by Venus – The heart chakra acts like a fulcrum between the lower physical chakras and the top chakras that are more associated with intangibles like compassion, love, ability to dip into the limitless powers of the Universe etc. The heart chakra ruled by Venus reflects your ability to manage love both in terms of giving true love and receiving love in all forms from others around you.

The heart chakra is the first chakra that makes us realize there is more to life than mere food, clothing, shelter, and other materialistic pursuits. Love is, perhaps, the first and the most powerful emotion that tells you there are spiritual realms beyond the senses of human beings. Love is also that drive that can compel you to achieve those higher realms.

In ancient texts, this chakra is given the power of creating the sound of a clap with just one hand. This one example can tell you a lot about the visual powers of our ancient sages. When you give love, you are creating a connection with someone else without expecting anything in return. Isn't that clapping with one hand? The only reward you certainly get with or without asking is the 'feel good' factor both you as a giver and the other person as a receiver of love gets and that too unconditionally.

The unfortunate thing is by giving love, sometimes people get hurt and this hurt causes a deep chasm in their hearts. Driven by this deep hurt, many people sadly block out the heart chakra out of fear of being vulnerable. The sad thing about deliberately blocking out the fourth chakra is you are also closing doors to all forms of love. This is a dangerous situation as you run the risk of becoming a cold automaton instead of a warm person.

Moreover, when you close the heart chakra, you are in effect closing out all the higher chakras as well because without the opening of the heart chakra, you will never know the existence of other chakras in your body which have the power to take you to bigger and more beautiful planes than you can imagine.

The Throat Chakra Ruled by Mercury and Jupiter – People with a robust throat chakra can be very persuasive people with amazing oratory skills. Such people seem to have the ability to pull out the thoughts from your head and convert them into compelling words and ideas.

The power of this chakra is its ability to empower you to speak what you believe in with great conviction. The ability to speak the truth you believe in gives you the power to create your own reality and identity. Call on the power of Mercury and Jupiter and enhance your communication skills so that you become your own person and create your own identity.

The Third Eye Chakra Ruled by Neptune – People with a powerfully open and transparent third eye chakra are very imaginative and easily create visuals even of seemingly abstract concepts such as those in Physics and Algebra. The power behind these imaginations is the ability of these people to feel and take in and absorb incoming messages through dreams and intuitions.

People with powerful third eye chakras usually see the entire vision which they then break down into small parts to recreate it again in their minds. When the image in the form of a dream or an intuitive picture appears in the depths of their minds, they feel compelled to put in the required efforts to actualize their vision.

Even people who are on drugs are able to see these images. However, as they are not in control of themselves, these images simply appear and disappear as disturbing concepts and patterns which they cannot clearly see and definitely cannot recall well enough to be compelled to work towards making these images a reality.

Pray regularly, regularly indulge in sessions of listening to yourself and your subconscious mind, and keep a log of these thoughts. They are wonderful ways of empowering the third eye chakra and making it more receptive to intuitions and insightfulness. Give yourself quiet moments when you can listen to the voice of the spirits and those men who have achieved higher realms and yet are making efforts to connect to people on our plane. You need to be receptive to these voices and for that, you need to give more power to your third eye chakra.

The Crown Chakra Ruled by Uranus – This is the energy center of your body and soul. When you activate this chakra, you can easily see the entirety of God's (use Universal Power, the Power of Nature, or anything else if you are uncomfortable using God here) will in one vision.

However, activating the power of this chakra calls for keeping a perfectly balanced system of other chakras so much so that the power of each is completely under your control. Letting go of your ego is the ultimate sacrifice needed to activate the power of this chakra. This can take place only when you are fully committed to the purpose of your life on this Earth. It is the final realm crossing which you will transcend human intelligence and abilities and become one with the Supreme Universal Power.

CHAPTER 8:

PROBLEMS THAT SOME OF THE CHAKRAS MAY ENCOUNTER

There are times, though, when your chakras may be blocked or imbalanced. This often happens because of emotional upset, caused by either accidents, conflicts, or any form of loss. There are also times when you get overly stressed and anxious and, in turn, your chakras suffer. When this happens, harmony is lost, and one may suffer from certain diseases or problems. Here are some of the problems that could lead to blockage of the chakras.

Root Chakra

The Root Chakra suffers when you feel like you cannot protect or cover your basic needs, or when you feel like you cannot put your necessities in order. When this happens, you get to feel like your prostates are affected, and feel problems in your feet, legs, male reproductive parts, and the immune system. These could then lead to eating disorders, sciatica, knee pain, and even degenerative arthritis.

To get this back in balance, you have to start believing that you have the right to be on earth and that you have an important role to play. Once you get this back in balance, you'd feel grounded, supported and connected to the world.

Solar Plexus Chakra

When your self-esteem is low and when you feel like you cannot believe in yourself, your Solar Plexus Chakra suffers. It also suffers when you fear criticism because of being criticized too much in the past, or when you don't feel good about your physical appearance.

When that happens, you may experience digestive problems, high blood pressure, liver dysfunction and problems in the colon and intestines.

In order to get this back in balance, you have to make sure that you accept yourself—no matter who or what you are; or what you can and cannot do. When that happens, you'll be able to have more self-respect and compassion, and you will be more confident and assertive.

Sacral Chakra

The Sacral Chakra is affected when you cannot express your emotions well, and when you cannot stay committed. It is affected when you fear things too much when you give in to your addictions, and when you betray yourself and the people around you.

These then cause urinary problems, sexual and reproductive issues, low back and pelvic pain.

In order to get this back in balance, you should allow yourself to take risks, stay committed and stay creative. You also have to learn to be passionate, outgoing and positively sexual. Once that's done, you'll easily be able to honor others—and yourself.

Heart Chakra

When you love people to the point of suffocation, your heart chakra suffers. It also suffers when you become overly jealous, bitter, and angry or when you abandon others without notice. This then leads to heart diseases, asthma, lymphatic system problems, breast cancer, shoulder and upper arm problems, as well as wrist pain.

You should then get the heart chakra back in balance by always letting joy, compassion, and gratitude rule over your life. You should also learn to let forgiveness flow and learn to give trust, as well.

When that happens, you'd learn how to love—whether yourself or also the people around you.

Third Eye Chakra

The Third Eye Chakra is said to be the most complicated, and not the easiest one opened. When you get too moody or let your emotions cloud your judgment, this chakra is affected. This is also affected when you daydream too much and let your imagination burn reality down. More than that, it is blocked when you forget to reflect on the state of your life, and when you become volatile—in whichever way possible.

In order to stop the blockage, you should learn to look at the big picture instead of overanalyzing things. Once this happens, you'll be able to have some clarity; you'd be able to focus on things that need your attention, be able to recognize fears and not let them take over your life and get to learn from others, as well. This way, you'd gain more insight and wisdom—and get to appreciate life more.

Throat Chakra

The Throat Chakra gets to be blocked when you cannot speak or write about your thoughts clearly, and when you feel like others are dictating what you have to do for you. In short, you'd get to feel as if you do not have any choices at all. This could then lead to a sore throat, thyroid issues, facial problems, ulcers and ear infections, together with neck and shoulder pain.

In order to get this back in order, you have to make sure that you let your voice be heard and that you speak your mind. When this happens, you'll be able to be honest and firm, expressive, communicative, and also be a good listener.

Crown Chakra

Finally, you have to understand your crown chakra. This gets blocked when you always try to find greater power than you have, and when you have problems using your knowledge and skills efficiently. Sometimes, it also gets affected when you let political and religious problems bother you too much when you carry prejudices against others when you over-analyze, and when you are scared of being alienated or being alone.

In order to stop this from being blocked, you should be able to live mindfully and have some clarity of mind. When this happens, you will easily be able to live in the moment and have the kind of wisdom and inner guidance that's unshakable and true.

Now that you know what blocks each of the chakras, you should now be able to live your life in such a way that you won't think too much—and that you'll always let peace and harmony reign in your life!

CHAPTER 9:

REMEDIES FOR DAMAGED CHAKRAS

You don't need a psychic to help you repair your damaged chakras. You can do it yourself! There are easy techniques to do so, and you have a lot of alternative remedies to choose from if one of the techniques does not work.

First Chakra

The biggest challenge for the root chakra is fear—so you need to develop courage, and realize that you're meant for bigger and better things. For that, you could use these affirmations below:

1. Hug someone, or ask someone to embrace you. This helps you become more grounded.
2. Rub your lower back for about 15 minutes. Do the same with your buttocks.
3. Lie in a very comfortable bed. A comfortable sleeping place will renew your energy.
4. Keep a plant in your home and take care of it. The soil will make you connect with Mother Earth.
5. Cook your favorite meals.
6. Begin your day with dancing.

7. Take a walk, preferably barefoot. It's a good grounding practice. It will take away any stress that you feel.
8. Have a picnic.
9. Recite mantras or affirmations with the following terms: health, security, responsibility, honesty, fairness, routine, organization, work, order, flexibility, and honesty.
10. Your power statements are "I need, I want."
11. Say any of the following statements:

I am a peaceful, divine being of light.
I am protected. I am peaceful and secure.
I am connected to my body; I am deeply rooted.
Just like a star or a tree, I feel safe and secure.
I have a right to be here on earth; my presence certainly means something.
I stand for justice, and truth; I stand for my values.
I can stand on my own two feet; I am grounded and stable.
I am grateful for the challenges in my life; I have the capacity to overcome them.
I trust myself and make choices that are healthy for me.
I trust in the goodness of life; I trust that the choices I make will help me grow and transform.
I love my life, and I trust myself.

Second Chakra

Being your body's passion and pleasure center, the main challenge here will be guilt, which can only be combated by taking risks—and by believing in yourself. Here's what you should do:

1. Get a good and relaxing massage. Reflexology will help loosen up the knots that you feel, not just physically but also emotionally.

2. Practice aromatherapy. Whether you are using candles or incense sticks, take time to smell the natural essences, and let them fill your lungs with renewed vitality.
3. Take sensual baths with Epsom salts. This kind of salt cleanses away the negative energy around you, purifying your chakra points.
4. Eat chocolate. Chocolate is an anti-depressant and is rich in antioxidants.
5. Work with clay or wood. Get your hands working with nature's best art resources.
6. Get a good haircut and feel good about yourself.
7. Feel the vibrations around you. Attune yourself to the sounds and sights, to the secret messages of the universe. Feel the connection between you and the soil, you and the flowers. Feel the energy coming from your fingertips. Put your hands over your crystals and feel the warm energy pouring forth from your palms.
8. Bake bread. Kneading distracts the mind and the heart, and the smell of pastry is good for you.
9. Take care of plants in your house. Bring nature to your indoors.
10. Relax in a rocking chair.
11. Write love poems and write love notes to someone.
12. Clean your house to get rid of negative and unwanted vibes.
13. Spread love and cheer to other people. The good energy will bounce back to yourself.
14. Say a mantra with the following terms: passion, love, vitality, desire, comfort, pleasure, beauty, sexuality, and indulgence.
15. Say the following affirmations:

I enjoy my body; I love my body.

I have healthy boundaries; I know how to take care of myself, and of my body.

I am open to using my senses in order to experience and appreciate the present moment.

I am appreciative of every breath I take; I have a lot of pleasure in my life.

I value and respect my body.

I am allowing myself to experience pleasure.

I am open to touch and be touched.

Emotions are the language of my soul.

I know that my sexuality is sacred; I vow to take care of it.

I am at peace; I can take care of my physical body.

Third Chakra

The main challenge that the Solar Plexus Chakra faces is how you can be aware of your personal power, and how you'll be able to use it in a way that's balanced and fair. In short, you have to be consciously responsible, and you have to be able to react to the circumstances in your life in the right way.

To do that, it's best that you do the following:

1. Protect your solar plexus chakra by folding your hands over it when someone angry is speaking to you. Doing so blocks the negative energy coming from that person.
2. Pretend to be someone you dislike so much so that you will know what it is like to be in their shoes. You don't have to go overboard; just knowing how they feel is enough.
3. Express your anger. You can write, punch a bean bag, cry or scream in the shower. Use whatever method of catharsis is available to release your pent-up emotions.
4. Act in the theater. Channel someone else's personality. Be other people for one day.

5. Throw a costume party at your house or be a cosplayer.
6. Know what your mission in life is. This will give more depth to you as an individual. You will become more aware of your purpose, and all your actions will have direction.
7. Your affirmations should be about focus, commitment, dedication, faith, choice, courage, discipline, autonomy, willingness, cooperation, and authority, examples of which are as follows:

I seek opportunities not only for personal but also for spiritual growth.
I love and accept myself.
I know how to choose the best for myself.
I honor myself.
I feel my own power.
I direct my own life.
I am worthy of respect, kindness, and love.
I am strong and courageous; I can stand up for myself.
I am proud of all my achievements; I know I did my best to deserve them.
I am free to choose in any situation.
I am authentic.
I am at peace with myself.

Fourth Chakra

The Heart Chakra is able to move through your life. It's able to help you get in touch with yourself and appreciate life better—and that's why its biggest challenge is grief. You then have to use affirmations to improve this chakra, and so you could live your life to the fullest!

1. Be someone's secret admirer. It doesn't have to be the romantic kind. You could admire someone for the way

they talk, dance, cook, or write. Learn to appreciate the talents of others.

2. Write yourself a love letter. What do you want to tell your sixteen-year-old self? Write that down, including admonitions and inspirational messages.

3. Apologize. Acknowledge your faults and shortcomings.

4. Build a spiritual family. This family will help you through rough times, especially when you need help in taking care of your spiritual needs. Your spiritual family could consist of your relatives, friends, colleagues or people from your church.

5. Look at your baby picture. Remember that you have an inner child. Don't strive to be a perfectionist.

6. Adopt a pet. This is good for the soul because you learn to take care of others.

7. Stretch on the bed, or do yoga.

8. Connect with nature. Take care of plants in your house. Put your hands under running water. Stand in the shower for several minutes as you relax your mind.

9. Create a gratitude list. Thank the universe and God for giving you your desires.

10. Create an altar. Put whatever you feel is important to you and always pray at that altar.

11. Create a "desires box". This is where you put all your wishes and desires. Write them on a piece of paper and do your best to achieve them within a year. Turn them over to the universe and believe in the power of the universe to grant your wishes.

12. Say the following affirmations:

I am open to love.
I accept myself completely and deeply because all love resides in my heart.

I am wanted; I am loved.

I nurture my inner child; I believe he is still and always will be important in my life.

I can forgive myself, and I always will.

I love and appreciate animals; I love and appreciate the natural world.

I accept things as they are.

I am one with the animals and one with nature; I feel a sense of unity with the world.

I am connected to other human beings.

I am grateful for all the challenges in my life.

I am open to kindness; I am always open to life.

Fifth Chakra

Throat Chakra is one of the most spiritual chakras. This inspires you to be creative and expressive—as well as being honest with yourself. Its main challenge are lies—you have to be able to see through them and, at the same time, make sure that lies will not rule your life.

1. Have a good and positive motto. For example, Today, I will speak kind words to people. The good chi that you feel will also be channeled towards other people.
2. Think that something positive will happen every day. Don't expect bad things to happen.
3. Breathe deeply and listen to a variety of sounds. Close your eyes and hear the sounds of the birds chirping, the cars passing by, the neighbors chatting.
4. Avoid complaining for one whole day and accept any criticism thrown at you.
5. Sing. This beats those unwanted energies. You will instantly feel good, too.
6. Learn a new language. It doesn't matter if it's French,

Spanish, or Japanese. It's cool to learn another set of cultures and symbols.

7. Let go of the past. Let go of the emotional baggage that holds you back. Wear a black obsidian gemstone if you have to.

8. Practice saying things in advance, especially when you think you don't feel comfortable in a situation.

9. Empower yourself with the mantra "I am." Complete the statement with any adjective you want to say. You could say, "I am strong. I am powerful."

10. Take a chance. Give people the opportunity to speak to you. Grab opportunities for change, too.

11. Keep yourself from retorting. It only brings bad vibes.

12. Then, don't forget to utter the following affirmations:

I am honest in my communication; I am open, and I am clear.
I can communicate my feelings with ease.
I have a right to speak my truth.
I can resolve my life's challenges through a strong will.
I can express myself through art, writing, and speech.
I have integrity.
I live an authentic life.
I nourish my spirit through creativity.
I am at peace.
I take good care of my body.
I realize my truth my listening to what my mind and body say.
I express gratitude towards my life.
I know when it's time to listen; I do not deny it.

Sixth Chakra

The Third Eye Chakra is also spiritual in the sense that you can appreciate both your inner and outer worlds. Your main challenge here is an illusion. You have to know how to blur the lines between reality and fiction; you have to learn to live in the real world, while still being able to use your imagination.

1. Watch good and beautiful films.
2. Look at a beautiful work of art, or place one at home or on your working desk.
3. Create your own greeting cards.
4. Place a bowl of fresh fruits near you.
5. Have a professional photo of you taken at the studio of your choice.
6. Create a mood board and visualize all the dreams and ambitions that you have in life.
7. Have a meditation garden. Plant/place all of your chosen plants and flowers here. Go here if you are troubled or if you want to meditate.
8. Attach magnets or any inspiring notes and photos on your fridge.
9. Train yourself to see auras. Relax and adjust your eyes until you see a colored halo above the head of another person. Do this often and you will begin to see auras in no time.
10. Your affirmations should contain the following words: invention, memory, clairvoyance, daydreams, insight, visualization, and open-mindedness. For this, you could try the following affirmations below:

I am the source of my truth; I am the source of love.
I am at peace.
My life is able to move effortlessly.
I am open to inspiration; I am open to bliss.
I am connected with the universe's wisdom.
I know that all is well in my world.
I love and accept myself.

I forgive myself.
I forgive the past; I make use of its lessons as guiding stones in life.
I trust my intuition.
I listen to the wisdom of my elders.
I nurture my spirit.
I am intuitive and wise and connected with my inner guide.
I try to understand and learn from my experiences.
I listen to my deepest wisdom.
I am in touch with my inner guidance.

Seventh Chakra

You have the crown chakra, which helps you become selfless and unite with every part of your body. Its biggest challenge is an attachment. You have to see things as passing things—as things that just come and go in life, the way most people do.

This way, it will be easy for you to accept change—and understand that it's really the only constant thing in life. Here are the affirmations you could use:

1. Compose a story about your past life. It could be funny, serious or scary. You will notice some similar points in your life until you realize that that same story explains your very fears and your personality.
2. Listen to classical and Baroque music.
3. Cancel out all the negative energy from the food you eat, or from the objects you hold.
4. Rest on Sundays.
5. Talk to the Higher Being, whether it is God, or Allah, or the Nature Goddess.
6. Allow the sound of a bell or a chime to resonate in your body and in your home.
7. Be a philanthropist and help the needy without asking

for anything in return.

8. Don't forget the following affirmations below:

I am at peace.

My life moves with grace.

I am open to divine wisdom.

I am connected with the universe's wisdom.

I know that all is well in my world.

I accept and love myself.

I am grateful for all the goodness in my life.

I live in the present moment.

I am open to letting go of my attachments.

I trust my intuition.

I listen to the wisdom of the universe.

I seek experiences that I know will nourish my spirit.

I cherish my spirit.

I seek to understand and learn from the experiences I've had in life.

I honor the Divine within me.

I am part of the Divine.

By using these affirmations, you'll be able to improve the state of your chakras—and experience a life that's full of love and peace.

CHAPTER 10:

CRYSTAL HEALING FOR CHAKRAS

Crystals could definitely make your chakras better— especially if you know the right ones to use, and that's why you should never leave them behind. When crystals are placed directly over your chakras, they're able to give off divine healing energy that is released through the energy channels in your body. This then makes its way to the aura and changes it for the better.

So, which crystals should you be using, then? Here's what you have to keep in mind!

Root Chakra: Garnet

Garnet is deemed as the crystal of the Root Chakra. As it is in the color red, it works with the Root Chakra because it's able to keep you inspired and grounded. It helps you become motivated to achieve your goals in life and to make sure that you do your best whatever happens.

Since it is in the color of Red, you kind of get the sense that it's perfect for awakening the first of your chakras. When you start with this one, you get to make sure that everything else will flow smoothly.

With the help of Garnet, you'll be connected to the earth—you'd be able to fight addictions, material desires, and being attached to material things—because life is so much more than that.

Sacral Chakra: Carnelian

Next, you have Carnelian, which is known as the best crystal for the Sacral Chakra. It gives you a better understanding of humans, and human life, as a whole. More than that, it's also able to hone your creativity, give you emotional balance, and help you have unity with yourself and with the people around you.

It is important to tap into this chakra with the help of Carnelian so that you wouldn't have to feel like going against the flow brings you nothing, or that you won't feel like you are working for nothing. You'd always be at peace; you'd always be motivated.

Solar Plexus Chakra: Citrine

Solar Plexus is responsible for your connection with the astral world—and even with your own astral body. When it's out of balance, you might be hypersensitive and overly emotional.

With the help of Citrine, you would be able to neutralize the negative energies that you have in your life. You'd be able to protect yourself, and normalize mood swings so that you'd be more appreciative of what's going on in your life. More than that, you'd also be able to let abundance and success be in your mindset so that you'd be motivated to do your best to achieve what you want. It will end your depression and self-doubt—and help you become a much happier individual!

Heart Chakra: Aventurine

Green Aventurine is the best crystal for the heart chakra. It's always good to take care of the heart chakra because it's quite sensitive. When not given enough attention, it may cause you to feel separate from others. It prevents you from loving people unconditionally.

However, with the help of Aventurine, you can bring things back in order. You'd be able to set realistic goals and remind yourself to do your best in order for them to come true. It calms you down and prevents you from being angry or irritated at times when you have to remain composed. It heals circulation and helps you be more in touch with yourself, balancing male-female energy in the process. And, it also promotes compassion and empathy; it makes you understand you're not the only important person on earth; others matter, too.

Throat Chakra: Jolite

Jolite works with the throat chakra's main color of blue. It's a crystal that makes way for clear expression, and also keeps the lines of communication open. When it works with the chakra, it's able to help you figure out what's right for you, and tell you what you need to feel inside.

Jolite is able to help you speak from the mind and from the heart—and not just one of them at a time. It's able to help you speak your truth so that everything in your life would easily flow, and you'd be able to manifest positivity in any part of your life. Jolite is also able to promote leadership, power, self-confidence, and inner strength—helping you express yourself way better than before!

Third Eye Chakra: Amethyst

Not only is amethyst one of the most popular stones out there, but it's also essential for the improvement of the third eye chakra. You see, when the third eye chakra is out of balance, you will find it hard to meditate and attach yourself to your inner being. You might also have an irrational and intense fear of death and may make you depressed for quite a while.

As Amethyst is known as the stone of meditation, it has natural calming and healing qualities. It's able to bring harmony, peace, and calmness in your life. It also develops intuition, increases your attention, and helps you train your mind to make lucid dreaming possible. Aside from that, it gets rid of compulsive behaviors—and always makes you feel at peace with yourself, with the world, and all the other beings in it.

Crown Chakra: Rainbow Moonstone

And lastly, you have a rainbow moonstone for the crown chakra. The colors pink, purple, and white are predominant in the crown chakra, so it's just fitting that a colorful crystal is also used for it.

As the name suggests, people believe that the rainbow moonstone has some connections to the moon and that it has quite some magic of its own. The said magic allows you to open up your heart and mind to spiritual development and helps you appreciate spiritual experiences. It helps you forget the illusion of time and allows you to be calm while making use of ancient wisdom to rule over your life.

How to use the crystals

In order to use the crystals, make sure that you go to a quiet place and put your hands on the table. Keep the palms near one another, and ask a friend to go hold the crystals above your arms, and to point and rotate them. When you feel some tingling sensations, that's when you'd know that the healing energy of the crystals is working.

If the moment feels too overwhelming, feel free to take a break and put the crystals away a bit. Then, repeat the process again.

Good luck!

CHAPTER 11:

USING JOURNALING TO SPEAK THE TRUTH AND HELP YOUR THROAT CHAKRA

For this one, we are going to spend some time talking about your throat chakra and how it is so important to helping you to keep the lines of communication open. Many times there are things in our lives that will make us not communicate well because they cause the throat chakra to close up a little bit. Not telling the truth to others, keeping out information that is important to the other person to make good decisions, or hiding our true identities because we want to impress other people can all get in the way of our throat chakra working in the proper manner.

Getting started with journaling

For some people, the throat chakra is going to be pretty closed up. They may be shy or anxious about talking to other people because of various things that have happened in your life. The idea of talking out to other people and trying to speak up in different social situations, much less try to show your true side to other people can seem really intimidating to these individuals. Yet, they still need to have a chance to speak the truth to open up their throat chakra so that they can start communicating again.

One method that you can use to open up the lines of communication a bit if you are dealing with anxiety or shyness is to get started with journaling. In fact, this can be great no matter how open or closed your throat chakra is feeling right now. This allows you to have an open and safe place to talk about your feelings, your problems, or anything else that is going on in your life. Since there isn't an issue with others seeing the information, you don't have to worry about the judgment of other people.

Those who journal a bit each day, often talk about how much better they feel. They are able to get some things off their chest and feel better in no time. They don't have to worry about the judgment and they can talk about whatever they would like during that time. It is a great way to speak up and you can use it to help you speak up to other people as well.

If you decide to get started with journaling, the process is pretty simple. You can choose to write out the journal with pen and paper or you can use your computer and write it all out. Then set aside about ten or fifteen minutes each day, preferably at the end of the day so you can sort out some of the thoughts that you dealt with during the day.

Turn on a timer and then just get to writing for the time you allotted. You don't need to worry about what you are writing, about grammar, or anything else. The only important thing here is to write down whatever is prevalent in your mind at that moment and just keep writing for the ten or so minutes that you set up. No one else is going to see the information that you are writing down, so get out of that anger, those secrets, or anything else that has been bothering you for some time. If you are able to keep up with this for a few weeks, you are sure to see a big difference in the openness of your throat chakra and you will be able to communicate better than ever with those in your life.

Other ways to speak the truth

While journaling is a great way to get all of this started out, it is now time to learn a few other options that you can work on to speak the truth to others. Your throat chakra is all about communicating and telling the truth. When you are too busy trying to protect the feelings of another person or you decide to lie because it will save you from getting into trouble, you are not telling the truth. This can cause a lot of damage to your throat chakra because you are not providing it the care that it needs.

If you have trouble speaking up to other people or telling them the truth, it is time to work on your throat chakra before the rest of your communication starts to fail.

The first thing that you can do is telling others the truth. Any time that someone asks your opinion about something or asks you a direct question, you should answer them truthfully. Often we feel that telling a little lie is not a big deal, especially if it is going to help us feel better or will prevent the other person from feeling upset, but this is really a dangerous way to be. You are not going to feel good over the long run for lying to the other person, and once the other person finds out that you have been lying to them, you are going to end up hurting them more than ever as well.

It doesn't matter if you are protecting yourself or another person by the lies that you tell when you tell a lie, it ends up harming you and the other person. This can close up the throat chakra and can close up your communication. The more lies that you spread around, the more that you have to watch your back and this can really shut down your lines of communication.

Keeping things hidden from other people, such as with lies of omission, can be bad as well. You may think that you are helping out the other person, but in reality, you are hiding pertinent information that they need to make some good decisions for themselves. This can cause as much damage to your throat chakra as any other types of lies, and you should always be open and honest any time that you are talking to others.

Another thing that you may not have considered when it comes to this is being true to yourself. Many times we will meet new friends or another person and we will want to seem really cool or to show ourselves off in a certain way. We will pretend to be someone we are not just to impress this other contact. This can be damaging to our throat chakras as well because it prevents us from being the people who we should be. It is always important to be ourselves no matter what company we are in, to ensure that we are keeping the throat chakra open and to ensure that others are really getting a chance to learn who we are.

Being open and honest with the other people you meet in your life is the best way to help you keep your heart chakra nice and open. It is easy to tell lies or omit information in order to try to make ourselves or another person feel better, but this is not the way to get things done. It is always best, to be honest with others, and to show our true colors and personality, all of the time to prevent issues with communication with other people.

CHAPTER 12:

HOW TO PRACTICE LOVE FOR YOURSELF AND OTHERS TO OPEN UP THE HEART CHAKRA

The heart chakra is a very important chakra that you need to work on. If you are not able to feel love for other people, it is really hard to feel whole. As humans, we are social creatures and we need to feel and give love in return for this to work. If you aren't able to keep some of the relationships that you feel are important to you and you have trouble showing your love to others, even though you feel like you should be showing this love, then it may be time to work on your heart chakra a bit.

Practicing love is one of the best things that you can do to help take care of your heart chakra. You don't need to make this something complicated, but changing how you act and some of the words that you say on occasion can make a big difference. Some of the ways that you can practice love in your daily life with others include:

Love isn't just about the feelings

There is a lot more that comes with love than just feelings. If you attach all of your love to a feeling, that is going to make it change based on your mood or the day, which makes the love very conditional, and that is not what love is all about. This is why there is more to love than just the feelings that you have. You need to make it so that your love is never based on the thoughts and feelings of someone else, but that it is something that is constant and around no matter what.

Your love is supposed to be unconditional, whether you are giving it to yourself, giving it to someone else, or you are receiving it as well. It is not tied to a behavior, to some words, or something else, you just give and receive love no matter what.

Adapt how you love other people

Love is often given and received in many different ways. And this is where there could be some issues between people. There isn't one way to give or receive love that will be the same for everyone, and if you find someone who doesn't accept love the same way that you do, it could lead to some confusion along the way.

This is why it is so important to realize that you need to adapt the love that you have for others. Just because you like to receive love in a certain way, doesn't mean that someone else is going to find it loving. You need to learn what the other person finds as loving and then work to show them love in that way, even if it isn't the same way as you find love in your life.

Learn how to love yourself

If you are suffering from issues with your heart chakra, this is most likely the reason why. We are so busy trying to show love to other people, to show them that we care and that they are important to us, but we spend very little time taking care of ourselves at all. In the long run, this is going to come back to haunt us and can make it difficult to really show love to other people because we are lacking in some ways.

For those who like to make others happy all of the time, which is something that many people are, you will probably spend most of your time trying to give love to those around you, but you will spend very little time trying to giving yourself some love. This love that you share all over the place with those around you will end up not being unconditional if you follow this path It is always best to save some self-love back for yourself, because this allows you to feel good about yourself all of the time, no matter how the other person changes or acts to you.

Love will sometimes feel uncomfortable

Another thing that you will have to realize when it comes to love is that it will sometimes be a bit uncomfortable. Too many of us feel that when we love someone else, whether it is a significant other, a family member, or a friend, that things should always be easy. But in order to really love someone, you need to be able to get through some of the rough times as well, rather than just giving up.

Pain and growth are actually a big part of your life and if you are trying to shield yourself and the other person from these pains and growth, you will find that you are not really showing them, love. There are going to be times when the two of you go through some rough patches. There is going to be times when you or the other person will experience some pain. And it is important that you let them go through these tough times while being there to support them so that the one you love is able to find their own way and learn how to grow.

The good news is there will still be times when your love will be happy and things will be good. But trying to protect from all the bad things that happen in life is not really unconditional love. You have to trust and believe that the one you love will be able to make it through the rough spots and your love will come out stronger than ever before.

Learn forgiveness

There is a fine line that occurs here. Forgiveness is not all about allowing someone to stomp all over you and do whatever they would like, but it is about learning how to react in a kinder way, in a way that is better for yourself, no matter what the other person did to you.

If you have run across the situation where someone has let you down a bit or has hurt you, it is always better to choose to forgive them by letting go of some of the resentment and the anger that are around you. How you will act towards that person, no matter who they are will change depending on the situation that has happened, but if you decide to let go of the negative feelings and to act lovingly, you are showing that you love the other person unconditionally.

Show love to everyone

It is so important to learn how to show love to everyone. It is especially important to show love to those you think don't deserve the love. Normally, if you are dealing with someone who is showing some negativity to you, it has very little to do with you personally and a lot to do with something else that is going on in their life. Often these people are having a big issue with learning how to love themselves.

When this starts to happen, it is important to take a deep breath before you react and learn how to put yourself in their shoes. This will help you out with your situation because you will be able to better figure out why they are acting in a certain way. You may then be able to show them more love without feeling slighted about the way they are reacting to you.

In addition to showing love to the people who may not deserve it at first look, it is also important to show love to all of the other people who are in your life as well. You want to make sure that you show love to your friends, your family, your significant other, your coworkers, and so much more. There should never be a limit to how much love you have to share with those around you.

Pick a simple act to show love each day

You should try to find a time each day where you can do a simple act for someone else to show them how much you love them. You should do some action that will help someone else out, but don't expect anything else in return. If the other person does reciprocate, that is great, but you should not be expecting it when you perform the action in the first place, or it doesn't seem loving. You can keep it pretty simple, such as letting someone get in front of you in heavy traffic, opening up the door for someone, or calling someone to tell them how much you love them.

There are so many different little actions that you are able to do for other people to show how much you love them, it is just about being deliberate and showing them that you really care. You should do one of these actions each day, if not more, without needing anything in return, and you are sure to get a huge amount of pleasure from giving out this love to others.

The heart chakra is really one that you should spend some time on. Too many times in our modern lives we are often not showing any love to the other people in our lives or we are not willing to show love in our own lives. But when you try to learn how to heal the heart chakra and to make it stronger than ever before, it is easy to feel love and to give it out as well. Make sure to check out some of the tips in this chapter and you will be able to send and receive all the love that your heart chakra needs.

One of the hardest things that you can do in your life is learning how to love yourself. Many of us are familiar with loving others and making them happy, but very few of us are familiar with how to make sure that we are happy in our own lives. Once we are able to learn how to balance the two, it becomes much easier to take care of the love that our chakras need to be happy and healthy all the time.

CHAPTER 13:

THE EFFECT OF YOGA ON CHAKRAS

If you may recall, it was mentioned earlier that yoga, especially tantric yoga, have resulted from chakras. Therefore, yoga could be a good way of awakening, balancing, and providing remedies to your chakras in the event that they get to be damaged.

According to Tantric Yogis, yoga is able to help you improve your chakras because it helps you experience a certain difference in your life. This way, you would feel the change coming from within.

You see, yogis believe that chakras resemble spinning wheels, because they involve a convergence of thoughts, feelings, and energy, together with their physical bodies. When this happens, you'll be able to separate reality from your emotions, be able to separate confidence from fear, and separate desires from aversions. When you practice yoga, you'll be able to unravel any blocks that may hinder you from tapping into your highest potential.

Here's how yoga can help each of your chakras:

Root Chakra

The center of this chakra is found on the pelvic floor. It makes you connected to the earth, as it is the root of your soul. It keeps you secure and physically strong—and helps you stay in touch with reality—and bring awareness to your center.

As it is the realm of fears and avoidance, you'd understand how your urges would revolve around food, sex, sleep, and survival. It also holds your most latent potential. This means that when you do yoga, you'll be able to breathe life into the root's sleeping power. The best poses for this include the Chair Pose, Warrior Pose, hip openers, squats, and lunges.

Sacral Chakra

Meanwhile, your Sacral Chakra is your water center. This is not only the home of your reproductive organs— but it is also the home of your desire. It's important to take care of this chakra because if not, your life may be ruled by attachments— and that is often unhealthy.

Once you do yoga, you'll be able to make sure that your consciousness will be able to move freely and that you'll be able to access your potentials to make way for sensual pleasure and healing.

For this, you could try deep lunges, asanas, forwards lunges, hip openers, and the Chair Pose, as well.

Solar Plexus Chakra

Next, you have the Solar Plexus Chakra. This is often associated with individual power and purpose, as well as one's passion and fire. This holds a vast amount of your vitality. When this chakra is blocked, you might have problems with your ambition and with gaining physical power.

However, when you're able to do yoga and certain exercises for this, you can be sure that you'd feel the energy of transformation work around you, and that your consciousness would now be able to move freely, too!

The most recommended poses for this are the yoga twists— they definitely can heal the solar plexus!

Heart Chakra

In Himalayan Tradition, this chakra is believed to be the most powerful of all. Some even consider it to be the very seat of one's soul. This is the meeting ground of all emotional experience.

Once you do yoga, you can be sure that your heart chakra would radiate the highest aspects of being a person, which includes compassion, total faith in the Divine, and finally, unconditional love. This will also help you deal with your deepest insecurities, loneliness, and disappointment.

In order to open this up, you have to make use of backbends and *pranayama* meditation.

Throat Chakra

As the throat chakra is associated with the element of ether, this helps control your metabolism. It is the home of hearing and speech.

With the help of yoga, you'll be able to tap into your spiritual self—and make sure that you develop a better relationship with the Divine.

The best exercises for this are asanas, the Fish Pose, the Shoulder Stand, the Camel, and the Plow.

Third Eye Chakra

Being the command center of the chakras, this is important in regularizing the energy streams in your body, especially where the mind and body converge. It is connected to your development and growth because it works directly on the pituitary gland.

With the help of yoga, you'll have relaxed consciousness, and also be able to improve your intuition; you'd understand that you are more than just a physical body and that you have an important place in this world.

The best practices here are the Chair and central breathing exercises.

Crown Chakra

And of course, there is the Crown Chakra. Almost any kind of yoga pose works great for this, and with their help, you'll be able to let go of your individual ego, understand your personal and linear needs, and also be able to process your emotional experiences. This way, you'd be on your way to extreme personal enlightenment!

CHAPTER 14:

USING MEDITATION TO HELP YOUR CHAKRAS

One of the best things that you can do to help heal your chakras is to add to daily meditation. It doesn't matter which chakra you are working on, though the third eye chakra will benefit the most, you will find that you can align the chakras and help them to work the proper way. If you feel that any of your chakras are not in good working order, it is time to add in some daily meditation, even if you only have five to ten minutes to devote to this each day.

Meditation is not something that has to be really difficult to get started on. You just need to have a quiet room, a few minutes to yourself, and the ability to relax and think about your chakras so that they are able to heal themselves. You can choose how you want to work on the chakras. Some days you may just want to work on the third eye chakra or another one that has been causing you the most trouble, and other times you will want to focus on all of them, helping them all to align with each other.

Now, there are a few different methods that you can use in order to get started with meditation. Here we are going to look at the method that you can use that is meant to specifically help take care of the chakras and will help to get them in line. But if you have never had a chance to get started with meditation and you are a bit worried about what to do, you can go with a traditional form of meditation, or simply work on just controlling your breathing and taking a break from the stress in your day to day life.

To get started, make sure to find a room that is quiet and where you are able to be by yourself without someone coming in to bug you for at least ten to fifteen minutes. You may end up needing a longer period of time, but this is a good place to start for your first few sessions. You don't want to have a bunch of distractions showing up during the meditation or you will have a lot of trouble getting the meditation to work well for you.

Once you find the room you want to use for your meditation, a room where you can be all by yourself during this time without interruptions, it is time to get comfortable. For the chakras to start realigning again, you need to make sure that you are sitting up straight so that they are all in order. This means that slouching is a bad thing and you need to be able to keep your back nice and straight during this. Sitting on the floor with your legs cross and maybe a pillow under you for some support is usually the best to get a good spinal alignment, but if you have trouble with being on the floor or some back problems, you can sit up in a chair; just make sure your feet are flat on the floor and that you are still maintaining good posture.

When you are ready, it is time to close your eyes and just concentrate on your breathing for a bit. You will want to just let your mind clear out for a little bit of time, working hard to not think about anything else for a few minutes as you try to get a bit of inner peace and away from the stress in your life. We will move on in a second to find how to work with the chakras, but it is really hard to focus on the chakras and to get them in the right order if you focus on the stress and challenges that you face in your daily life. So spend a few minutes, or as long as you need, clearing out some of the things that are bothering you and stressing you out before you move on to the next step.

Now, it is perfectly fine if you would like to stay at this step for a bit. Some people find that clearing out some of the stresses of their lives and just taking a breather can help them out with cleaning their chakras. There is so much more that you are able to do, but getting started with some deep breathing and relaxation will help you get so much further in the long run. You can always stick right here for now, and then move on when you feel more comfortable to do more for your chakras.

If you would like to work on your chakras and move further into the meditation, you can do this as well. Here you would need to focus on the colors that are associated with the different chakras in your body. You can choose to just focus on the chakra that is causing you the most trouble, or a really good meditation session would ask you to focus on all of them together to make them stronger and to make sure they are all in good working order.

First, concentrate on the root chakra, or the first chakra. Remember that this one is located at the base of the spine and it is linked to your connection to the world and to other people. This one is going to be associated with the color red. When you want to work on the root chakra, you will want to get started with meditation and then focus on the color red, letting it get brighter and duller and just focusing your energy on it until it begins to envelop you all over. You can take as long as you would like on the root chakra so don't rush the process.

Next is the sacral chakra, or the second chakra, which is right below the navel. This one is linked to your innocence, creativity, and your inner child and when you are thinking about this one, it is all about the color orange. When you are done with the root chakra, it is time to move to the sacral chakra and focus on the color orange, going through the same process as before, focusing just on the orange color until it begins to envelop you as well.

When you are done with this one, it is time to work on the solar plexus, or the third chakra, which is going to be a little bit below the heart and down to the navel. This one is all about your reaction to criticism and to your self-esteem. To work with the solar plexus chakra, you will need to focus on the color yellow. Make sure to work with it for as long as needed until the color yellow starts to surround you again.

The heart chakra is the fourth chakra and you will be able to find this one right in the middle f the chest. It is linked to a lot of your emotions such as trust, openness, compassion, and love. It is sometimes associated with pink, but for this meditation, you will want to focus on the color green. When you are done with the solar plexus chakra, you will move on to your focus of the heart chakra with the help of the green color, letting it get nice and bright for you.

Next on the list is the throat chakra or the fifth chakra. This one is located near the base of your throat and it is going to be linked to expressing the truth, personal authority, and even taking responsibility for your own needs instead of blaming someone else. When you are focusing on the throat chakra, you will need to focus on the color blue. So when you are done, working with the heart chakra, it is time to change over to the color blue and let that color surround you as well.

The brow chakra, or the third eye chakra, is found right at the center of the forehead. It is the one that you will need to work on when you need help with intuition, wisdom, inner vision, and more. This one is going to resonate with the color of indigo so that is the color that you will need to focus on if you want to help the brow chakra to work better.

And finally, you can also work on the crown chakra or the seventh chakra. This one is located at the very top of your head and it is associated with living in the now, your awareness of Oneness with the Source, and more. If you need to work on this one, you will be able to focus on violet as well as pure white light, so you can focus on the one that makes the most sense to you. Allow this one to focus for a bit until the color has surrounded you.

You get to choose how you would like to get this done. It is preferable to work on all of the chakras together because this helps to keep them aligned and working together properly, but there are sometimes when you need to get it done and since working on all of the chakras can take sometimes, you may want to shorten up the process a bit. Working on one or two of the chakras in a session to help you get started, and to save some time, will work out just fine and can provide some good benefits as well.

In addition, it is possible to work with all of the chakras at once. This is one of the best ways to ensure that your chakras are going to stay in good working order for a long time, so you need to make sure you have plenty of time to get this all done. Then you won't feel rushed and can slowly go through all of the chakras, giving each one the amount of time and attention that it deserves to work properly.

Remember that when you work on meditation, it is not a race or a competition. You don't want to feel bad because it takes you a bit to clear your mind and get the results that you want. Some people will pick this up faster than others and some will need a bit more time to perfect the skill.

If you do have some issues with working on meditation, be gentle with yourself. It is not a good idea to get angry or frustrated with meditation because this can cloud your judgment and takes away from some of the hard work you are doing. During this time you are supposed to use the exercises to help you focus on the chakras, or at least focus on relaxing and getting away from the stresses of the world around you. If you end up being upset about your lack of progress, you are defeating the purpose.

When your mind does end up wandering away from the exercises that you are working on, just gently bring it back to the task at hand. You want to be gentle, not bringing out any judgment or getting angry about what is happening at all. Things happen and if you focus your energy on these exercises and work at it, over time you will be able to get it down and you will get the best focus possible while doing your meditation.

When you are able to take some time to work on all of the chakras together, you are making it easier to get them all aligned at the same time. It is fine to work on a little bit at a time if this is all that you have time for, but it is best to spend some time on occasion, perhaps every few weeks, to help you realign all of the chakras that are in your body.

CHAPTER 15:

VISUALIZATION OF YOUR CHAKRAS

For some people, the reason that they are not able to get their chakras under control is because they are dealing with too much stress. Stress is just a normal part of our modern world today. No matter what you are doing in life, there are going to be times when you are dealing with a lot of stress that slows you down. You can be in charge of so many things in your daily life, from taking care of the kids to working on going to school and so many appointments each day. It is no wonder that most people feel a little bit stressed when it is all said and done.

Stress is one of the biggest reasons that your chakras are going to be out of line. There is so much that can go wrong with your chakras when stress comes into play because stress will take over all parts of your life. Stress can make you tired, can make you focus too much on one thing, can ruin your heart health, and so much more. Learning how to get rid of some of the stress that is in your life can make a big difference in how well your chakras are going to be able to work for you.

One method that you can use to help get your chakras back in line is visualization. This is a good relaxation technique because it allows you some time to break away from the stress and chaos that is in your life because you get to focus on something that is much more relaxing for you in the first place. Even if you are only able to spend about ten minutes on this each day, you are going to see results from that short little break.

This method is similar to what you will find with meditation, but some people prefer to go with visualization because it allows you to have something to focus on rather than just your breathing. It allows you to focus on a picture or a scene that is meant to relax you. You will get to pick out the picture or the scene that you are working on so there isn't any pressure and you can change it out as much as you would like. This is part of the fun when you work on visualization because you will get the chance to mess around a little bit and find what works the best for you.

If you would like to get started on visualization, the process is pretty simple. You will first need to schedule in about ten to fifteen minutes of free time each day. The time of day is not so important, but it is important that you can be let alone for that amount of time. Consider scheduling it in so that you won't have to worry about running out of time during the day or forgetting to get it done when things get a little bit crazy. You may also want to consider having a timer nearby. It can get really distracting to always think about how much time you have left before the visualization session is over and the timer will be able to track everything for you so that you won't have to worry about it and can just sit back and relax.

The next step is to figure out what you would like to spend

your time visualizing. Each person is going to be different so take some time to think this part out. Some people may like the idea of being able to sit back and imagine themselves enjoying a nice warm cup of coffee on occasion and hearing the sounds around them. Some people may like the idea of getting to sleep in, sleeping right on their big comfy bed without having to get up or go take care of things. Some may like the idea of walking on the beach and feeling the waves crash all around them. There are so many different visualization pictures that you are able to go with, but the important thing is that you find the one that is really relaxing to you so that this all works.

Once you have your picture or your scene ready, it is time to begin. You will want to turn on the timer and then sit down in the quiet room, paying attention to your posture along the way. Close your eyes and try to shut out all of the other things that are going on in the world around you and just focus on what is going to happen next. When you are comfortable and calm, perhaps taking in some deep and slow breaths for a few minutes ahead of time, it is time to bring out that picture that you want to use for your visualization.

Remember that you are able to use any picture that you would like, but here we are going to use the picture of walking on the beach for relaxation. When you are ready, pull up the picture of that beach and focus on that. You are going to want to look at a lot of the tiny details about this picture and about why it helps you to relax. Don't worry, there isn't a test when this is done and no one is going to be checking on you, but having a good idea of some of the details can really help to complete the picture and will give you some better results when you are done.

Imagine yourself on the beach, walking on the sand. Does the sand feel hot from the warmth of the sun all day, or is it a little bit later in the evening and it has begun to cool down a little bit? Do you feel the sand as soft or is it a bit rockier as you walk along? How does the wind feel on your shoulders and your hair or is it earlier in the day and you get the benefit of the full sun right on your back? How does all of this feel to you?

You can also move on to some of the sounds that are around you. Are there a lot of big waves that come crashing down around you, or is the sea and ocean pretty gently to mess with right now? Do you get the benefit of being at the beach all by yourself or are there a lot of other people who are showing up with you? Can you hear what they are saying or are they just a little bit of the background noise that is around you?

It is also possible to think about what you are doing when you are on this beach scene. Are you walking along the beach for the whole time or do you like to sit back and just watch what is going on around you? Are you someone who likes to sit under an umbrella and just relax at the beach or do you want to get out there and swim a little bit. What are you wearing when you are at the beach and how do the clothes feel against your body? What about your drink? Does it taste good and cold on this hot beach day and is it providing you with the hydration that you are looking for?

When you are doing the visualization, you are able to focus on any part of the image that you would like. You will find that the fifteen minutes will go by really quickly and you may only have time to feel the sun, the wind, and the sand from the first set of questions. If this is enough to relax you a little bit better than before, then just stick with this part and go to imagining this each time you work on your visualization. If you would like to mix it up a little bit more, you can switch over to imagining different parts of the scene each day that you do this visualization technique.

After the fifteen minutes are up, you can take a few more deep breaths and then go back to getting some of your work done or starting the day, depending on when you did the visualization. You should already feel so much calmer than you did before starting this session, even if it is just the first time that you went through and did this. Think about how relaxing and energizing this will feel if you are able to save aside the right amount of time to make it happen each day.

The reason that this works so well is that you are able to take a break from all of the things that are stressing you out. Sometimes just trying to do the deep breathing from meditation is going to frustrate people who aren't able to turn their minds off. Meditation can be amazing for helping you to reduce your levels of stress, but if you are someone who can't get your mind to shut off, it may not be the right option for you. Visualization still asks you to slow down and stop thinking about what is going on during the day that is stressing you out quite a bit, but it gives you something else to focus on, which can be more effective in the long term.

You are able to choose the image that ends up working the best for you. We talked about the image of being on the beach here because it ends up being a really relaxing option for a lot of people. But you can choose whatever one you would like, just make sure to go through it kind of like we did for the beach. Explore the different things that you hear, the sensations that you are feeling, what you are eating or drinking, who else is there with you, the touch of the fabrics on you, and so much more.

Don't rush through this process at all. It is meant to be relaxing so if you spend the whole time worrying that you are going to miss something or that you need to get through a certain part of the image before the fifteen minutes are up, you are going to miss out on the relaxing part of this technique. If you need to spend more time on one part on a certain day, that is fine. There are no rules for how quickly or slowly you need to go through this, just pick a pace that seems about right for you and stick with it. You want to feel relaxed when this is all over, no more stressed out.

When you are able to reduce the amount of stress that is going on in your life on a daily basis, you are going to see a huge amount of change that goes on with your chakras. Stress has the ability to knock out all of your chakras and make them feel like they are closed up and not working at all. When you follow some of the steps that are in this chapter about visualization and use them to help you to reduce some of the stress that is in your life, you will find that it is easier than ever to get those chakras to line up in the proper manner.

CHAPTER 16:

OTHER REMEDIES FOR YOUR CHAKRAS

Aside from the normal, mundane things that you can do to rebalance and repair your damaged chakras, you can try other techniques as well. These techniques may or may not work, depending on your lifestyle and preference, but you can definitely try all of them out to see what suits you best.

1. Meditation. Unblock your chakras by meditating. This is the most widely-practiced technique to repair your chakras. First, you have to be in a place where you are so comfortable. It should be quiet so that your mind will not be troubled. Do away with gadgets and accessories when you are meditating. As much as possible, be close to nature. Go to your meditation garden and sit there. Go out and walk on barefoot. Sit on the sand and feel the sea breeze. Surround yourself with rocks, stones, and crystals. Pray and talk to God. Don't forget to breathe deeply and exhale to release the tension in your body.

2. Rapid Eye Technology. Eliminate stress by mimicking REM sleep. Bury all your fears and anxiety deep in your subconscious and focus only in the NOW. This one should be

done with the help of a professional to help you out. This is not always the best option to use because it does require a professional to help you to get the work done properly. But for some people who need help getting rid of some of the issues that come with their chakras, you may want to try working with rapid eye technology.

3. Visualization. Also called creative visualization, imagine yourself as how you want it to be. Whatever dreams you have, you can achieve them by seeing yourself ten years from now, all happy, healthy, and wealthy. You can also visualize a white light surrounding you, enveloping you from head to foot, cleansing you of all the unwanted bad energies that you have absorbed from pollution, from people, and from objects. Imagine this white light swirling around you downwards and feel that the light is also making you feel lighter by the second.

4. Crystal Healing. Choose the gemstones and crystals that work best for your chakra and create a sacred space in your home where these crystals are together. You could also lie down and place the crystals on top of the chakra region you want to heal. Wear the crystals every day (as a bracelet, pendant, etc.) and notice the changes in your body and mood.

5. Yoga. Nothing could be more relaxing than yoga. It teaches you to relax and be one with your soul. It energizes your body while making your mind relaxed. Yoga is really good for helping you to work more on your breathing a little bit and it can be amazing for releasing tension, strengthening the muscles in your body, and helping you to feel better than ever before. There are numerous yoga poses that you are able to use in order to gain the cleansing of the chakras that you are looking for.

6. Emotional Freedom Technique. Your acupuncture points are tapped, releasing unwanted energies from these points. All of your pent-up emotions are released as well. If you would like to be able to use this technique, it is probably best to find a professional acupuncturist to help you out. They will be trained to know exactly where all of these points are in your body so they can answer your questions and help you to really see the benefits that you are looking for.

7. Reframing your beliefs. Condition yourself to a set of new standards or principles if the old ones do not work. Many times the reason that your chakras are not working the right way is because your frame of mind is not quite right. You may be someone who thinks about things in a negative manner. When things don't work out the right way, you are either frustrated or you are mad because that is how you expected it to happen, rather than taking that situation and learning from it. Sometimes having an outlook on life that is more positive can help you to open up the chakras. You are using this as a way to let go of some of the anger that is in your life so that you can feel happier and healthier in no time.

8. Drink a lot of water: some people believe that one of the best ways to deal with your chakras is to take the time to drink a lot of water. This can help to clear out the system and get rid of some of the toxins that are building up inside of the body. It can also help to clear your head so that you are able to make good decisions, and it can help you to feel happier. Adding a few more cups of water to your intake each day will make a big difference. In addition, cleansing yourself in water, usually in the ocean or with a salt water and baking soda bath for twenty minutes, can really help to clear up some of those chakras and makes you feel so much better.

9. Walk barefoot. This technique is otherwise known as communing with nature. Nature resolves our fears because we are part of nature ourselves. This is why, scientifically-speaking, you also feel good when you drink water after a confrontation. You suddenly feel calm. Externally, nature can do that to us as well. A lot of people do walks in the park or in the forest when they are angry or upset. Somehow, there is something about nature that makes us calm and collected. This method is going to help you to become more grounded in the world around you, which can be helpful when you are working on the first, or the root, chakra.

10. Self-examination and Reflection. This is new. Consider yourself your own priest or your own detective. You ask yourself a lot of questions until you bring yourself to the realization of a very important matter. These questions have something to do with your activities and behavior, how you conduct yourself when you are alone or when you are with others. The next chapter gives you an expounded version of these questions.

CHAPTER 16B:

OTHER REMEDIES FOR YOUR CHAKRAS PART 2

Sometimes you will see people wearing certain colors, more often than not, or you may see them wearing particular pieces of jewelry, such as stone bracelets, stone or crystal necklaces or something similar. At first glance, these people may simply appear to be making a fashion statement, or they may just seem to be a bit more ethereal than most people in their fashion choices. While this may be true, it is also possible that these people may, in fact, be practicing certain techniques to heal or strengthen their chakras. In addition to the 10 previous remedies for your chakras, here are a few more that you can practice on a daily basis without even needing to take any extra time or energy to do so.

1. Use the power of music to restore chakral health. The fact that each chakra responds to different vibrations is common knowledge. Mantras and vibrational chants are used to great effect in stimulating the energy within a given chakra, using different tones or chords depending on the chakra in question. However, music can be used to achieve the same results with equally great effect. Initially, you might expect meditation music or some other form of ambient sound

compilation to do the trick. However, the truth of the matter is that different genres of music can actually serve to stimulate chakral energy. This shouldn't really come as a great surprise, seeing as different types of music can affect your mood in different ways. Classical music, for example, might cause you to become more academically minded, focusing on your intellectual mindset. This is an example of you using music to strengthen your chakras without even realizing it. Any music that helps you to focus on intellectual matters will stimulate the energies of the Third Eye Chakra, that which is responsible for intellect and wisdom.

Any song that inspires you and makes you feel good about yourself is ideal for renewing the energies of the Solar Plexus Chakra. Most people have a particular song or two that serve to inspire them, and whether they realize it or not, that inspiration is nothing short of chakral healing and strengthening. Music that makes you feel relaxed and calm will address the Heart Chakra, the center of your sense of love and inner peace. This music doesn't have to be soft or calm in nature, it simply has to have a calming effect on you while you listen to it. Additionally, any music that inspires your creativity or your imagination will stimulate the energies of your Throat Chakra, the seat of communication and self-expression. Any songs that inspire a strong sense of self-esteem will also help to strengthen this chakra as well, as self-esteem and self-expression often go hand in hand.

More ethereal musical choices might inspire you to focus on the spiritual side of things, including the sanctity of life, the beauty of the world, or your connection to the universe itself. In this instance, the energies of your Crown Chakra are being invigorated, causing your mindset to open up to the higher energies around you. Again, if you have a song that has this effect, but is not what you would expect, such as a rock song, that doesn't matter. Whatever music has an impact on you is the right music to use. Therefore, take the time to create a list of songs that serve to improve your different moods or frames of mind. Figure out which songs stimulate which chakras, and develop a soundtrack that will help to nurture each of your chakras for when you need those energies restored.

2. Use color to restore chakral energies to their full health. You may find that you have a craving to wear a particular color at some point, maybe even for several days in a row. Even more telling, you may find that your closet is dominated by specific colors, accounting for half or more of the clothes you own. While this can be chalked off as simply being indicative of your favorite color there may, in fact, be a lot more to this than you might expect. In fact, the very notion of what your favorite color is may actually have a lot more significance than you might ever have imagined. After all, you probably never think twice about a person with a powerful personality, choosing red as their favorite color since red is regarded as a power color. The question is, why is red a power color?

When you take the time to look at the different chakras and their colors, a great deal suddenly becomes very clear. Red is the color of the Root Chakra, the seat of primal energy. While you might associate the Solar Plexus with power as it is the seat of self-confidence, the fact is that power is also a primal energy connected to our basest emotions. Thus, the Root Chakra will be the seat of power. Even so, the color yellow is only two colors removed from red and is the color of the Solar Plexus Chakra where assertiveness and self-esteem are housed. Therefore, when you consider the nature of the colors and their emotions, and you see how closely related they are to each other, suddenly the meaning behind colors takes on a whole new meaning. Instead of a person's favorite color simply being a random choice based on what is pleasing to the eye, it becomes clear that favorite colors actually represent a person's true nature. More significantly to this point, your favorite color represents your dominant chakra, the place you draw most of your energy and strength from.

Recognizing your dominant chakra through color preference is a good way to gain a deeper understanding of who you are. In the case of having a few colors that you prefer, you will discover that you draw energy from multiple chakras, each represented by one of those colors. This can be useful in determining your strong suits, such as confidence in the case of red or yellow, communication in the case of blue, or spirituality in the case of purple or white. However, there is another side to the coin which is vital to your chakral health. While you can discover the chakras you use the most by seeing the colors you use the most, you can also tell which chakras you use the least by discovering which colors are missing. If red is missing from your color scheme, then you probably aren't very grounded in earthly or primal matters, such as home, basic survival and the more instinctual emotions of trust, fear and the like. Thus, in the event that you want to increase the energies in the chakras that are missing from your color scheme, you will want to acquire items with those colors.

This doesn't mean that you have to change the color on your walls, however. Rather, it means that you can incorporate colors in a way that will strengthen certain chakras when you need them most. For example, if you have to give a presentation and you want to increase your communication skills, then wear blue in order to invigorate the energies of your Throat Chakra, the seat of communication. Wearing red when you are competing in a sport or contest will raise your primal energies, making you more competitive and eager. Alternatively, wearing green is an ideal way of soothing your mood and increasing the energies associated with the Heart Chakra, the seat of love and compassion. Wearing certain colors for certain events will help increase the specific energies you need for those events. In a way, it's almost like becoming the form of yourself that you need to be in order to ensure the best results.

3. Use specific stones to stimulate chakral energies. While the use of crystals and stones for chakral energy healing and strengthening has already been covered, one thing that remains to be addressed is the importance of personally making amulets for this purpose. The value of specific stones and crystals for chakral health is very significant, but what can make these things even more significant is when you take the time and effort to actually create a piece of jewelry or any other talismanic object for chakral healing. This makes perfect sense when you consider that the item you will use, whether it's jewelry or something else, will have the energy of its construction within it. Since this is all about energy, then every aspect of energy becomes vitally important. Therefore, while a red stone like a garnet will have positive effects on your Root Chakra, if you are simply using a loose stone it will have less of an impact than if you are using a piece of jewelry with added meaning. Stones put together on a necklace for the sake of healing the Root Chakra will be imbued with an extra level of energy that will make it all that much more effective.

In addition to jewelry or sacred objects having more energy than simple stones or the like, how the object is made will have a profound difference as well. While you might see a necklace that speaks to you, if it is made in a factory sweatshop overseas, then the energy in it will be less effective than if a fellow practitioner made it for you. Furthermore, the power of an object that you create yourself for a specific purpose is beyond any other form of object that you can find. The energy that you put into the object while making it will be with you when you use it, making it far more powerful and meaningful than any object you could find in any store. Thus, as well as simply using colored stones to improve chakral energies, take the time to create objects incorporating those stones for that purpose. This will ensure that you have increased energy, as well as guaranteeing that the energy is positive. The very last thing you need is to buy a necklace that was made by someone having a bad day. The negative energy in that necklace will take a long time to wear off, and that is something you don't want to have to deal with.

While jewelry and other accessories can help to strengthen chakral energies with specific stones or crystals, everyday decorative objects can also be used to very great effect. If you take the time to make a display using colored stones, such as a Zen garden, a water feature, or any other decorative piece, then you can turn any room into a virtual temple for any particular chakra. Bluestone objects will create an atmosphere that will energize your Throat Chakra, restoring your communicative abilities whenever you are in that room. Using different colors will have the same effect for the other chakras, meaning that you can even convert the same room simply by exchanging one color for another. Thus, if you know that you have to give a presentation several days in advance, decorate your living space with as much blue as you can. This will serve to strengthen your Throat Chakra whenever you are in that space, enabling you to be better prepared for the day of the presentation.

4. Use fragrance to stimulate chakral energies. The use of sound and color to cleanse and heal chakral energies is well known, so it should be no great surprise that scent can also play a huge role in this area. After all, just because the chakras represent your non-physical body that is not to say that they are wholly separate from your physical self. Thus, using the physical senses can go a long way to both hurting and healing chakral energies. The sense of smell is well known as one of the strongest senses with regard to memory and imagination. Simply smelling a pie can cause you to remember being at your grandparents' house years ago as a young child when a similar smell was coming from their kitchen. Such memories are rarely evoked with visual or audio cues. That said, the power of smell can have huge effects on chakral energies and overall chakral health.

One of the main practices in this area is the use of essential oils. Burning oils is an easy and inexpensive way to fill a room with a particular fragrance, thus creating an atmosphere of healing and wellbeing. Just as different chakras have different colors and sounds associated with them, so too they have different scents. While these scents are already listed in the book, this would be a good place to reference them again.

- Root Chakra- Patchouli, Frankincense
- Navel Chakra- Orange, Clove, Juniper
- Solar Plexus Chakra- Lemon, Peppermint, Rosemary
- Heart Chakra- Rosewood, Basil, Rose
- Throat Chakra- Sage, Lemongrass, Blue Chamomile
- Third Eye Chakra- Spruce, Clary Sage, Lavender
- Crown Chakra- Myrrh, Sandalwood, Geranium

Using these essential oils in addition to yoga or meditation is an excellent way of maximizing the results of your efforts. If you focus on a specific chakra on a daily or weekly basis you can coordinate the colors in your room, the yoga or meditation you practice, and the fragrances you use in order to create a complete approach to restoring the energies of that particular chakra. Playing the appropriate music as well will involve every physical sense in the process, ensuring the best results possible.

While essential oils are a great way of creating the necessary fragrances they are not the only method for achieving that goal. Many chakras have herbs and natural plants as their fragrances as well, meaning that you can grow these plants in your home, thereby creating a perfectly natural source for the fragrances needed. In addition to using these plants for their fragrant qualities, you can also use them as flavorings for your food. Thus, if you are trying to increase your communication skills, then adding sage or lemongrass to your food will help to stimulate your Throat Chakra, increasing its energy levels and improving your ability to express yourself clearly and effectively. Again, this is an all-natural way to integrate the healing properties of these plants into your day to day life, thus creating a healthier lifestyle for your overall chakral wellbeing. Additionally, the smell of cooking with natural herbs will create a lasting impact on your environment that will affect your chakral health for days on end.

5. Seek the help of a professional healer. So far all of the remedies for strengthening and healing chakras have been largely self-reliant, meaning that you can do these things on your own. However, there is another form of healing that may be of equal if not greater effect. That is the use of a

professional healer. While you might feel a bit nervous about using another person to help restore your chakral energies, consider how it would sound if you only resorted to self-healing techniques for physical ailments. While treating a common cold or allergies can be easily done without doctors or hospitals, the fact is that there are certain times when proper medical care will be necessary. The very same holds true for matters of non-physical health. Just because you understand the basics of chakral energies and how to influence them doesn't mean that you won't need extra help from time to time. And there is certainly nothing wrong with asking for that help, just as there is nothing wrong with going to a doctor when the need arises.

One example of when you should seek extra help is when you feel as though your efforts aren't producing the desired results. If you are using all of the techniques available to the best of your abilities and still aren't seeing any change in your condition, then it is probably time to bring in extra help. While there are a great many people out there who are scam artists, there are also a great many people out there who are legitimate healers with very real abilities. Finding the right person may take a little extra effort, but it will be well worth it in the end. Ask anyone you know for recommendations, as word of mouth is the most reliable form of advertising there is. Additionally, try to stay away from anyone who is 'over the top' in their appearance. You will intuitively know if someone seems a little too showy in their advertising, and it is important to listen to that intuition.

While it might take some extra courage to trust another person with something as personal and intimate as your chakral health, bringing in a competent healer can make all the difference in the world. The first benefit is that you will have the knowledge and experience of that person to help you to get back to proper chakral health. This is critical since you may not be experienced enough to accurately diagnose a particular problem. Their experience will help speed up the process by finding what is wrong quickly and thus enabling you to start on the road to recovery that much sooner. Another huge benefit is that you will have the energies of that person to work with in addition to your own energies. When multiple people focus their energies on a particular thing they increase the results many times over. Thus, having that extra energy can also help tremendously in getting your own energies in line.

CHAPTER 17:

THE 12-CHAKRA SYSTEM – PART 1

While most of the people look at correcting and adjusting the seven primary chakras in their lives, you must know that there are many more chakras that affect the way we live and how our life turns out. It is believed that there are more than 100 chakras that guide and affect us. However, as a beginner, it could be very confusing to learn and master all of them. Yet, it would be naïve to stop at seven too. Therefore, I thought it made sense to include the next level of chakra learning in this book and that is the 12-chakra system.

Being aware of the 12 chakras in your system will help you better understand the depth and appreciation of the working of the chakras than if you limited your knowledge to only the seven primary ones. You will be able to add nuances to the treatment process that will otherwise not be visible to you.

Explanation of the 12-Chakra System

Before that, a little recollection of what are chakras. Chakras are energy vortexes that exist everywhere in our body that have the power to absorb energy from the cosmos and again release the energy into the cosmos. The energy that is released is what comes out as reality.

These chakras or energy centers play a very important role in the well-being of an individual. The energy points have the power to influence a person's physical, emotional, and spiritual health. Therefore it is essential to try and achieve a balanced and open system of chakras. You have already been introduced to the seven basic chakras and the elements, colors, and other aspects associated with each of them. Now, let us move on the remaining five of the 12-chakra system.

The Five Chakras Outside of Your Body

The remaining five chakras of the 12-chakra system all lie outside of your body and yet have a powerful influence on you and your personality. These chakras are the ones that help us connect to the lower and higher astral planes beyond the five senses. These five chakras are believed to be capable of helping you link to those planes that your subconscious mind can reach and absorb energy.

While it may not be as easy to balance and access these five energy points as you can balance and access the seven primary ones within your body, it is possible to harness their energies (even for an average human being) and use them for improving the quality of your life. Also, remember that these chakras are the ones with the power to connect you to spirits and angels from the planes above and beyond the human realm.

Before we go into each of the five chakras, here is some more relatable information about the 12-chakra system. The basic logic behind the principle of the 12-chakra system is that all living beings are connected with each other through the entire universe and are part of a whole. Every one of us is connected to the earth below and the universe above through a thin cable stretching about 3 feet beneath the ground and hundreds and thousands of miles above your head reaching far out into the vast expanding universe. Using all the 12 chakras will help us draw energy that lies in these spaces and use them for our benefit.

Additionally, there are different forms of 12-chakra system that are used by different belief systems. This book deals with the following format:

The seven chakras already discussed in detail within the human body

The 8th, 9th, 11th and 12th chakra above the crown chakra reaching out to the universe

The 10th chakra below your feet reaching into the earth

Let us look at each one of these chakras in a bit of detail

Earth Chakra – the Eighth Chakra

This chakra is located about 1 inch above the crown chakra and when we reach this, we can transcend the limitations of time and space. This energy vortex is believed to give you access to parallel lives and universes beyond human limitations. This energy center is very useful for shamanic healing and is believed to help connect with spirit guides.

This center is known to be the seat of spiritual selflessness, spiritual compassion, and divine love. It is also the place where the karmic residue or the effects of your actions are held on for more than one lifetime. When you can activate this chakra, you are opening your heart and mind to an entirely new level of energy and awareness.

You will be able to sense that you are part of a much larger community than you believed until now. This seat of energy allows you access to ideas and capabilities beyond human frailties. With an open earth chakra, you can achieve body and spiritual projection. It is believed to be the gateway to things beyond this planet of ours. Therefore, the earth chakra is referred to as the last energy point that holds anything human in it.

Opening this chakra allows you to break free from elements that have rooted you to earth and you become ready to shed your humanity to achieve something much larger than humans can dream of. You begin to realize new levels of intuition and awareness. The biggest shock you will feel when you open the doors of this energy point is that you will have to let go of all human connections.

Now, depending on your karmic load carried in this center, opening this chakra could lead to friction that you find difficult to overcome. You will have to learn to deal with new and unexplored spiritual abilities which could lead to you feeling ungrounded and alienated from yourself. Although this sounds like magic, the effects can be quite scary and unless you are prepared for a new and totally unexplored journey and your karmic load is not aligned to this discovery, it might not be wise to go beyond the balancing and opening of the seven primary chakras in your life. Yet, when you reach this stage, any healing process will bring up past karmic traumas and you will be able to help yourself and other individuals through the healing process.

Mantras – There are two mantras that are used by most chakra practitioners to open and heal the eighth chakra. These two include 'ma-ah-zod' and 'dee-ee-oh.' Both these mantras when chanted diligently and with faith have the power to open up the eighth chakra and reveal its powers to you benefiting you and others around you.

Color – The color associated with the earth chakra is the ultraviolet light which is invisible to the naked human eye. An exercise you can use to open the powers of this energy center is to visualize a deep violet light with bands of green color spiraling around it.

The Ninth Chakra – the Seat of the Soul or the Lunar Chakra

This chakra is located about four feet above the crown chakra and opening this chakra allows you to access data that helps you know the true purpose of your soul. The energies in this chakra help us shape our destiny. It holds the karmic blueprint of the person. It is the place which holds all the learning, knowledge, and skills the soul has learned over all the lifetimes.

There are basically three types of karmic blueprints; the teacher, the healer, and the creator. The blueprint stored in this center will give you an idea of what category you are slanted towards as each blueprint type is different from the other two. For example, the 'healer blueprint' will have more lifetimes spent on learning and imparting healing skills. Similarly, the creator blueprint will reflect many lifetimes spent creating new things and the teacher blueprint will reflect a type that works far more intensely with humanity than the other two types.

These skills from previous births become very important as you become achieve increased spiritual progress. These skills come in handy to open and release energies of the higher chakras. All the past lessons are integrated into a wholesome blueprint helping the soul understand the true meaning of its human existence and what it needs to do to achieve the true purpose. That is when wisdom sets in. Opening this chakra will help you do just this.

However, here is an important point of note. All will be good if every skill and every aspect of learning has been put into the right perspective and gets into the blueprint without conflict or partial understanding. When this does not happen, that is to say, when some of the learning is not complete or is not put in the right perspective, then when this chakra is opened, the skills cannot really be tied together to get the correct picture of the soul's true purpose. The individual cannot ascend more and will be held back in such cases.

To overcome this block, it might be necessary to heal this ninth chakra. The healing process will help the individual be free from the limitations of incomplete learning and skills not clearly put in perspective so that he or she can continue the upward journey into the higher chakras.

For example, an individual with a healer blueprint might have incomplete skills in the teacher and/or creator realms. To complete the learning circle in a wholesome manner, this individual will need the skills of the teacher and the creator to come forth as well. Incomplete skills in the other two types will prevent this individual from ascending further.

Therefore, to overcome this, the ninth chakra for this individual will need to be healed. The actual reason for the block is quite immaterial as the healing process will take of it irrespective of the reason behind the incomplete learning. The healing process does not convert the incomplete learning into complete learning by tying up loose ends. It simply converts the learning into wisdom. When the ninth chakra is fully healed and the blueprint opened up for you to see, you will be able to view the detailed circuitry of your soul.

Mantra for healing – The mantra used to open up the seat of the soul or the ninth chakra is 'el-ee-tee.' The repetition of this mantra will help you remain locked up in the ninth chakra giving you the time and resources to work with it and unfold its secrets to you. Hold your heart chakra with one hand and your third eye chakra with the other hand while repeating this mantra.

When you feel a web of highly intricate circuitry, you will know you have reached the ninth chakra. Now, feel through and identify the improper connections and incomplete filaments in this web. When you find these improper connections, simply feel yourself correcting them and putting the wrongly wired filaments into their proper positions. After you have finished, check again to see if the energy you are feeling is right.

If it feels right, you have achieved the healing process. Withdraw to your normal state and continue your ascension. If it doesn't feel right, you could give it another try again later on. Go back to the healing process when you feel ready for it again.

You must, however, know that the healing process of this ninth chakra may not take too much of energy from you. In this high chakra, the filaments are already there and the only block is a few strands that are out of place. You simply need to find those misplaced strands, put them back in order, and return. There is no need to open and close this chakra as well. There is no need for any kind of balancing too. Therefore, energy will not be expended much in the healing process of this chakra.

Color – When all the filaments of the circuitry of the ninth chakra are healed and properly placed, the seat of the soul chakra radiates a colorful form of energy that looks like a rainbow. The color of the chakra depends on what learning or skill the individual is accessing from this storehouse of skills at that particular point in time. So, it is not possible to assign any particular color to this chakra.

CHAPTER 17B:

THE 12-CHAKRA
SYSTEM – PART 2

The Tenth Chakra – the Solar Chakra

When the tenth chakra is opened, you can not only access the skills of the previous births but can also manifest those skills in the present lifetime. When this chakra opens up, the barriers that exist between the various lifetimes will begin to break down and there will be seen a continuity in time and space. The knowledge and wisdom gained will flow through these open gates letting you access them and manifest them at will.

The tenth chakra, located about a couple of feet beneath the ground you stand on, is responsible for the merging of the female and male characteristics, for divine creativity, and to synchronize all lifetimes of your soul. Divine creativity is the ability to align all your life elements in perfect harmony with each other and as a whole.

When this harmonious life happens, all your efforts will simply fall into place. For an outsider who does not understand the level you have reached, it will look like everything you do happens only in a positive way. You will appear as if being a magician by getting it right every time.

Divine energy from the tenth chakra is flowing into your life and making everything perfect. Moreover, when you tap into the skills of previous lifetimes, there is no discrimination shown between the male and female lifetimes resulting in a complete merger of the two gender qualities. This merging of the two gender qualities simply enhances the perfection in your life.

Individuals who have been successful in tapping into the tenth chakra will neither appear overly feminine or overly masculine. There is a powerful sense of neutrality about them that gives them the freedom to tap into the best available skills needed to get things done perfectly.

However, it is important to remember that such people will simply not get up one fine morning and feel neutral. They will slowly and surely overcome their gender polarity and embrace the power of neutrality over time. If you are healing a person whose tenth chakra is in the healing process and slowly is opening up, it might be wise to advise the person of these gender changes that will inevitably occur over a few years and tell them there is nothing to be worried about and that they are simply closer to attaining spiritual wisdom than many others in this world.

Also, it might be a good time to point out that there will hardly be any changes in the person's sexual preference. It is not as if the person who was until now attracted to women will now be attracted to men. Those things will not change much. However, the person's ability to relate to both sexes will increase naturally as the masculinity and femininity would have merged through the opening of the tenth chakra.

There will be hurdles and problems that you will encounter

when the tenth chakra is opening. Here is an example of a typical problem. The ninth chakra contains the skills of the past life, right? Well, when the tenth chakra is opened, it is quite likely that the ninth chakra is still in the healing process. So, the filaments there are yet to be wired properly, but the tenth chakra is already opening up.

What happens can be quite disturbing. Because the filaments in the ninth chakra are improperly connected, the opening of the tenth chakra will be hindered as you cannot access the skills from the previous lifetimes that are stored in the ninth chakra preventing you from manifesting them in the present lifetime.

During such times, the healing of the ninth chakra should be focused on before trying to open and accessing the powers of the tenth chakra. Once this is healed, you can automatically access the skills and manifest them in the present lifetime as per the powers of the tenth chakra.

Moreover, the smooth functioning of the tenth chakra is what helps an individual to integrate skills into their daily lives. This is what synchronizing skills are about. For example, if a person is clearly skilled in something, but he or she is thwarted from manifesting that skill, then it is quite likely due to some disharmony in the tenth chakra.

There could be blocks in the tenth chakra that are preventing the manifestation of the skill. It is possible that some kind of fear from a past lifetime is causing the disturbance and it would be good to go into a healing mode to clear those fears from the person's mind before allowing them to bring the skills from there to their present lifetime in the most wonderful way possible.

The tenth chakra can be compared to the heart chakra, which

takes the energy from all the other six lower chakras and processes them in an efficient way. Similarly, the tenth chakra (of the higher chakras) takes the energy stored in all the other four points and efficiently helps you manifest them suitably in your daily life. The job of a well-performing tenth chakra is to integrate skills from everywhere and bring them to life in a harmonious and synchronized way.

Healing the Tenth Chakra – Holding the image of an intensely blue light while meditating is an effective way of healing this chakra. This helps in dispelling old fears that are deeply embedded from previous lifetimes. The blue light will help in soothing and remove all the rough spots and calms the individual which, in turn, helps in managing deep-rooted fears.

The mantra that can help in healing this chakra is 'zod-i-pi-di.' This mantra specifically helps in unlocking the balancing effects of the male and female characteristics helping you achieve a harmonious state.

The Eleventh Chakra – the Galactic Chakra

Although the unlocking of other chakras can take any number of years depending on various factors, including energy levels, your commitment, etc, the 11th and 12th chakras are bound to take the longest time to open up. The 11th chakra is the center that contains energy and the required resources to learn and master advanced spiritual skills such as teleportation, time and space travel, telekinesis, bi-location, etc.

You must remember, however, that the skills in this center have nothing to do with showing off some kind of magic. They are meant to help you achieve the required maturity and development to move into the next phase of ascension.

The skills are not meant to be used in cheap gimmickry for financial gain. If you come across people who do this, I would recommend avoiding following them as their maturity levels are in doubt and the chances of them failing are very high.

The eleventh chakra is beyond the materialistic limitations of space, time, and matter. It is that center wherein you can view the galaxy while still retaining your physical form. At this stage, the individual has already merged with the mother aspect of divinity (or the Soul with a capitalized S) and is all set to merge with the father aspect (or the soul without the capitalization).

The father aspect of divinity or the soul is a person's core being without a physical structure like the human body. The Soul (with the capital S) is the part of the self that is accomplished with all the physical learning and knowledge. An individual merges with the Soul sometime between the openings of the 8th -10th chakra.

The opening of the 11th chakra makes an individual become aware of his multidimensional self across other planes. This center of energy gives the person an indication of what to expect when he chooses to ascend further. He will be able to access himself not just on the physical plane but in other planes as well. The consciousness of the individual expands to include multiple dimensions.

It is important to open this chakra in a gradual and even manner. Otherwise, the person can be thrown into utter chaos and his or her inability to manage huge changes will result in lasting damages. Rose quartz or gently rose-colored light can help in opening of this chakra in a slow assured manner smoothening the entire transition process for the person.

Although the opening of this chakra is usually easy as the

previous ones are already open and ready, it is possible for some individuals to lose patience and push through in an aggressive manner resulting in chaos. An example of such a person is one who wishes to simply increase commercial profitability from his ability for amazing gimmicks. Such people will invariably not have the patience and the required restraint to wait for the right time to open the 11th chakra. This impatience could cost them hugely as the chances of the other chakras closing up and not responding to healing are quite high.

The eleventh chakra is situated about 15 feet above the crown chakra which increases the complexity of the healing process even further. Placing one hand on the solar plexus chakra and the other on the heart chakra, imagine rising up to reach the position of the 11th chakra. Feel the rose-colored light flow into this chakra. Keep using this exercise until such time the doors of the 11th chakra open up and the powers and energies are transferred to you.

Another problem with the 11th chakra is the way these powers are manifested. Ideally, the powers you gain from the opening of this chakra remain dormant until such time the 12th chakra opens up too. You will not be able to manifest the powers of the 11th chakra. Then, after you have managed to open the 12th chakra, you might be required to revisit the 11th chakra and rewire loose and wrongly connected filaments to remove any erratic consequences of a wrongly wired skill.

The rewiring has to be done in the same way that was discussed for the 9th chakra. The mantra you should use here is 'ni-pi-ta.' Repeat this mantra silently as you visualize the inner circuitry of wires in the 11th chakra. Identify the mismatched ones and feel yourself connecting them correctly.

Once the healing is done, seal the circuitry with the same rose light. Unlike the ninth chakra healing process, this will take time and energy. If a second healing is required, then you must ensure a gap of at least 6-8 weeks from the first healing process.

Remember the 11th chakra is a treasure trove containing spiritual sources that are waiting to be tapped. Accessing the contents of this chakra will help you combine the human and divine aspects of life in a harmonious manner. Connecting to the 11th chakra will create a powerful pulsating wave come from right beneath you, moving through your entire body while touching every chakra, and finally fading away into the wide expanse of the universe.

The 12th Chakra – the Universal Chakra

The Universal Chakra or the 12th chakra is a beautiful thing to behold. It vibrates like a multi-colored sun and can be truly experienced and appreciated only through the third eye or through the inner eyes of your mind. Like the sun, the brightly burning 12th chakra exudes light, energy, and warmth.

It is your personal sun and hides in it immense power and strength which if you can access will help you create new non-physical and physical dimensions. The energy in the 12th chakra can be used to bathe all the chakras below it so that they can be made to work more efficiently and effectively than before.

When this happens, the physical body simply disappears and what remains is only a light which means that the individual is in complete ascension and has the power to go to any part of the universe he or she pleases.

While the 11th chakra is feminine, the 12th is masculine. It is important not to confuse this masculinity and femininity to the human gender versions. Here, masculine means gross, vibrant, and outgoing whereas feminine means nurturing, loving, and more skewed inwards than outwards.

The 12th chakra is the one that releases the powers and the skills stored in the 11th chakra. It has the capability of taking the skills from the 11th chakra and transcending time and space to indulge in out-of-body experiences. Even teleportation and telekinesis can be manifest by the powers of this chakra though these require the complete ascension process to take place. Additionally, the 12th chakra powers can facilitate control over natural elements such as air, water, earth, and fire.

As the 12th chakra is the doorway to the cosmos, most of the powers here are for use in the space beyond earth. Problems with the 12th chakra could be related to wrongly wired filaments in the 11th chakra or other blocked ascension energies. When ascension energies are blocked, strange outcomes can be noticed including but not limited to disappearing objects, objects appearing suddenly, things falling down inexplicably, an ability to heal without limitations, uncontrolled inner visions that can scare you if you are not ready for it, etc.

This is how chakra experts explain such anomalies. The blocked ascension energies all accumulate and suddenly when it gets too much to hold, they burst forth and builds the momentum of the 11th chakra energies which results in unexplained outbursts and manifestations of skills stored there. This happens unintentionally.

While a healing session might help to manage this uncontrolled and unintentional accumulation of energy, the root cause of this is the fear of leaving earthly attachments and completely letting go. It is very likely that people who are feeling the effects of these ascension energies may not even realize it is happening. They only realize that changes are taking place and such inexplicable changes create fear and panic resulting in blocking of these energies.

The best thing to overcome fear at this stage is to know that accessing the ascension energies will not take you off from the planet overnight. It is only a beginning and it might take years to accumulate sufficient energy to do galactic transportations. By then, you would have anyway overcome the fear of this new energy and you would have gained skills to get back when you please.

It is also good to remember that you cannot ascend until you are completely ready for the out-of-the-world experience. Moreover, no one can ascend (with a one-way ticket) until their work on this earth is done. So, instead of restraining the powerful energies, simply allow them to flow through and relax in your present being.

Self-healing of the 12th chakra (or using the services of another healer) requires an immense amount of energy. Use any means, including meditation to achieve the highest spiritual state. Place one hand on the top of your hand and the other hand on your heart chakra.

The mantra that needs to be repeated is 'na-el-i-el' or 'nalel' which translates to 'Life flows from the highest river.' This mantra is a key to unlock the 12th chakra and allow the ascension energies to flow through your body, mind, and spirit. It also helps to keep the 12th chakra balanced.

It would be a good thing to perform a healing session of the 12th chakra every two months if you feel you have problems here. It might be important to note here healing of the 12th chakra happens naturally and no healing process is needed. Any healing process might simply help in hastening the effects of the ascension energy. If you simply leave it alone, the wrinkles and problems of the 12th chakra will heal themselves.

So, the 12-chakra system believes that outside of the primary seven chakras from the base of your spine right up to the crown, there are 5 other chakras that are not easily discernible to the beginner. This energy system of the 5 chakras is latent in everyone and as each one is opened and breached, the next one becomes visible.

The extended system of the 12-chakras is the next step in the evolution of your spiritual journey. While the seven primary chakras are meant to help you in the development of your earthly characteristics to lead a better and happier life than before, the balance 5 chakras that lie outside of your body are meant to break humanly barriers and transcend time and space and see parallel universes and your oneness with that Supreme Power that rules this universe.

The five chakras outside your body help you move away from yourself (or ego) to embrace and encompass other people, other realities, and finally, divinity itself. As you broaden your spiritual vision, you move out of your little well and are ready to step into the wide expanding universe to embrace all the energies. You are ready to step into alternate realities and see yourself in multiple dimensions simultaneously.

One of the first things that learning about the 12-chakra system teaches you is the fact that the earth and you are merely a minuscule part of this spectacularly huge universe.

It helps you break barriers of time and space. You realize that you have existences in other dimensions that are as rooted as your roots on this earth.

As the powers of these alternate realities hit you, you achieve a sense of maturity that was hitherto unprecedented in your life. You visualize a new picture wherein you see yourself as a little musical instrument that is contributing to the universal orchestra that is being orchestrated by the powers that be. Most importantly, you see yourself as a part and parcel of that Supreme Power and you feel eternally grateful for all the beautiful things and joys that are bestowed on you!

CHAPTER 18:

QUESTIONS FOR SELF-EXAMINATION

In the end, all of the techniques for strengthening and cleansing your chakras are of no value if you don't have a clear understanding of your chakral condition. It would be like going to get medicine when you don't actually know what is wrong with your body. The first thing you need to do is to assess your overall chakral health, thereby determining both the positive areas and the negative areas. Fortunately, you don't have to go to a doctor or a specialist in order to determine your chakral health. By simply asking several questions you can figure out which chakras are strong and healthy and which ones are suffering and need attention. Once you discover which chakras need help you will be able to make better use of the techniques presented in this book for chakral healing.

Since each chakra is unique in terms of its energy and function different questions will need to be asked in order to uncover the condition of each chakra. These questions will get to the heart of each chakra by focusing on the specific aspects related to the chakra. Thus, the root chakra will focus on matters of the family, the sacral chakra will focus on matters of expression and pleasure, and so on and so forth. The most important thing is to make sure that you answer these questions truthfully. This is not a matter of judgment or of trying to win, rather this is an attempt to discover any area where you need to improve your energies, thereby increasing your overall health and sense of wellbeing. Any dishonesty in these answers will only serve to slow progress down, which will result in you being needlessly kept from reaching your true potential. However, if you take the time to consider the questions carefully, and answer them truthfully, then you will be well on your way to improving your life in every way imaginable.

1st Chakra

As this chakra relates to your sense of grounding many of the questions will focus on aspects of your upbringing. The fact is that your parents established your life on this earth, thus their influence on you, both positive and negative, will go a long way to determining the wellbeing of your Root Chakra. Your sense of belonging to this world will also be revealed. If you have a healthy Root Chakra you will feel comfortable and confident being in this world. However, an unhealthy Root Chakra will lead to insecurity, defensiveness and even paranoia. Negative answers will indicate a need to focus on this chakra, using the techniques discussed in order to get rid of negative energy and restore positive energy. Positive answers, however, will indicate that you already have a healthy and happy Root Chakra.

1. What are the blessings that you have received so far?
2. What beliefs have you inherited from your family?
3. What behaviors were influences of your family?
4. What positive traits did you inherit from your parents?

5. What negative traits did you inherit from your parents?
6. What qualities would you like your own family to learn from you?
7. What is a personal code of honor?
8. What superstitions and principles do you have?
9. What makes you angry?
10. What makes you happy or sad?
11. Have there been any power struggles in the relationships that you had with people?

2nd **Chakra:**

Since the second chakra, or Sacral Chakra, is related to your emotions and creativity, the questions associated with this chakra will revolve around those attributes. They will address how well you interact with others, determining your ability to form healthy relationships. By answering these questions honestly, you will also discover how healthy your inner artist is. If your answers are consistently negative, then this is a chakra that will need a lot of work and attention in order to cleanse and strengthen its energies. However, if you answer most of these questions in a positive way, then your Sacral Chakra is healthy and vibrant.

1. What is creativity for you?
2. How would you like your creative space to be?
3. What is your best form of artistic expression?
4. What dreams do you want to pursue in your life?
5. Do you judge other people easily? Why? What do you feel afterwards?
6. Do you overly criticize yourself, calling yourself and other people names and other derogatory terms when you and they have failed in a task?
7. What are your addictions? How do you address them?

3rd Chakra:

Questions about the Solar Plexus Chakra can be the most difficult to ask. After all, this chakra is the seat of your sense of self. Thus, anyone with low esteem will have a tough time with this list of questions, as they will reveal their insecurities rather quickly. Still, as stated before, it is absolutely critical that you answer these questions honestly. The only way to improve low self-esteem is to recognize that you have it in the first place. Having the courage to face that fact is the foundation of developing a stronger sense of self-worth, which will improve your life beyond measure. However, if your self-esteem is already strong these questions will be easy to answer and will reveal a healthy and robust sense of self-worth.

1. Do you like yourself?
2. Do you need the approval of other people?
3. Are you happy with what you have achieved so far?
4. Can you speak the truth in a calm manner?
1. 5, Are you afraid of confrontations? If not, how do you handle them?
5. Can you communicate your concerns easily?
6. Are you ready to handle responsibility?

4th Chakra:

Determining the health of your Heart Chakra, or 4th chakra will go a long way to helping you to establish healthy relationships on a more intimate level. Since the Heart Chakra is the seat of love and compassion, ensuring its health is vital to building and maintaining healthy personal relationships. Having a strong Heart Chakra will also enable you to have a healthier outlook on society as a whole. Alternatively, a weak or damaged Heart Chakra will cause countless problems with creating or maintaining relationships on any level. Negative answers to these questions will doubtlessly reveal the cause of emotional frustrations. Fortunately, now that you know how to fix a weak or damaged Heart Chakra, you will be able to make things right in no time! If, however, you have many close and healthy relationships in your life, then you will probably answer positively to many or even all of these questions.

1. Do you still have emotional baggage? How do you try to let them go?
2. What issues in your life need to be remedied?
3. What fears do you have?
4. What is your understanding of forgiveness?

5th Chakra

The health of the Throat Chakra, or 5th chakra, is the basis for your ability to communicate with others. This communication is as much about your ability to express your opinions as it is about the opinions themselves. Being too strong-willed can lead to issues of judgment that can be as devastating as being weak-willed or unable to communicate. If you are able to express yourself clearly without hurting other people's feelings, even if you disagree with them, then you have a healthy Throat Chakra, and you will answer these questions positively. However, if you tend to step on other people's toes, or you have a hard time getting your opinions heard, then your answers will probably be more negative, indicating a need to strengthen this chakra.

1. Are you strong-willed?
2. Where do you get your strength?
3. What do you do with your weaknesses?

6th Chakra

While the other chakras have been primarily associated with your relationship with the world and other people, the Third Eye Chakra, or 6th chakra, is associated with your relationship to the divine. Regardless of what religious upbringing you have had, the chances are that you have a very strong belief in one form of divine energy or another. This belief is critical to your ability to handle situations beyond your control. After all, being able to cry out to a protective being is instinctive, just as a child calls out to their mother in a time of distress. If you have a strong and healthy belief in the divine, then you will answer these questions in a positive way. However, a weak or fragmented belief system is indicative of a struggling Third Eye Chakra. Thus, if you answer these questions negatively, then finding your faith will be of the utmost importance.

1. How spiritual are you?
2. What rituals do you do to connect with the Higher Being?
3. How do you connect to your inner psychic?

7th Chakra

Finally, there is the Crown Chakra, or the 7th chakra, located at the very top of your head. This is the seat of your understanding and knowledge, as well as your ability to transcend and obtain enlightenment. If you constantly feel bogged down in the day to day life, then this chakra is probably weak or damaged and will require extra attention in order to bring it to its rightful place. However, if you have a strong sense of understanding, regarding both basic and higher concepts, then your Crown Chakra is probably very healthy and strong. This chakra is your connection to the

159

higher levels of consciousness, just as your Root Chakra is your connection to the earth. Thus, ensuring the health of this chakra is critical for improving your overall sense of spiritual wellbeing.

1. What insights do you have for today?
2. What meditative experiences did you have?
3. Do you have significant dreams lately?

As mentioned earlier, the most important thing is that you answer these questions honestly. After all, if you cheat on these questions, you will only be cheating yourself. Thus, honesty is essential for discovering the areas in your life that need the most care and attention. It is also essential that you take the necessary time over these questions. Give each chakra the time it deserves, being careful not to simply rush through these questions for the sake of getting them done. Most of the remedies for weak or damaged chakras listed in this book involve patience and a calm frame of mind. If you apply those same attributes to answering these questions, you will achieve the best results for your efforts.

CHAPTER 19:

THE SCIENCE
BEHIND CHAKRAS

When you hear talk about chakras the first thing you associate them with is probably spirituality. After all, the concept of chakras has its roots in ancient India, the very personification of spirituality if there ever was one! From Hindu gods and goddesses to the origins of Buddhism, ancient India covers a wider spectrum of spirituality and religious tradition than just about any other place or culture on the face of the Earth. Modern-day forms of meditation and yoga owe their very existence to the mystics and healers of the subcontinent. Therefore, it is no wonder that the tradition of chakras evokes such a rich and reverent sense of spirituality. However, there is another side to chakras, one which is more modern and certainly less spiritual, at least at face value. This other side is the science behind chakras.

Modern science has produced countless discoveries in terms of the human body and the role that energy plays in our very existence. While the concept of energy is certainly nothing new, the quantification of energy definitely is. Never before have we been able to actually see and measure the amounts of energy being generated by a living thing. With today's science and technology such feats are now commonplace. In fact, much of modern medicine utilizes the ability to measure and monitor the energy levels within the human body, thus determining the health and wellbeing of an individual in ways that the ancient mystics of India would have doubtlessly understood all too well. After all, the idea that energy makes up all living things is something we might consider revolutionary in scientific terms, but it is very old news to those who have been practicing chakral health and wellbeing. Indeed, the knowledge that we have obtained through modern breakthroughs in technology has done little more than validating the ancient traditions of chakral energy and their role in human life.

One of the first things to recognize when it comes to the science behind chakras is the significance of just where the chakras are located. Placing the energy centers of the subtle body along a central axis makes good sense as they are more balanced and centered along that line. However, you could ask why chakras weren't placed below the Root Chakra position, at the knees or feet for example. Alternatively, you could question why chakras were not allocated to the hands. After all, what part of the body is more associated with energy than the hands or the feet? Yet the seven main chakras are contained within a short span, traveling up the central axis of the human body along the spinal column. And here is where the science behind chakras begins to take shape. It turns out that the spinal column is, in fact, the conduit through which electrical impulses are transmitted from the brain to all other parts of the body. The nerves which run through the spinal column are virtual telephone lines, bringing every sort of message from the command center of the brain to all other parts of the physical body. Thus, the spinal column is nothing short of an energy highway, seeing energy flow from the brain to the body and from the body back to the brain again.

The fact that the spinal column is the path for energy to flow throughout the body would be enough to get anyone to consider the validity of the chakras, regardless of their spiritual beliefs. However, this is not the end of the story. What is even more striking is that the locations of the lower five chakras correspond directly to actual nerve clusters along the spinal column. This means that not only did the ancients understand the function of the spinal column, but they also were aware of the significance of the nerve clusters along it! Just as the chakras are considered energy centers of the subtle body, the nerve clusters along the spinal column, five in total, are actually energy centers of the physical body. Some might argue that this is nothing spectacular. After all, if anyone studied a dissected body, they would see the nerve centers in the spinal column. While this is true, it must be understood that those same ancients had no modern equipment with which to measure the energy in those nerve centers. Thus, those nerves could have served any function to the casual observer. Yet the ancient Indian sages knew somehow that those bundles of nerves were, in fact, the centers of energy in the physical human body.

Perhaps this is a classic matter of which came first, the chicken or the egg? While it is possible that the ancients studied the anatomy of the body, it is also entirely feasible that their knowledge of the chakras had little or nothing to do with their understanding of the human body. We may never know what inspired their belief in seven separate energy centers along a central axis, but what we can be sure of is that their knowledge goes hand in hand with the knowledge we are only now beginning to acquire regarding how the physical body works. It is therefore entirely possible that the ancients were made aware of the workings of the subtle body and that only now can we see the direct correlation between our subtle form and our physical form. Either way, modern science, and medicine have only served to validate the concept that energy centers do in fact exist along the spinal column, and that the health and wellbeing of these centers greatly impact our overall physical health and wellbeing.

The five nerve clusters along the spinal column account for the first five chakras, beginning with the Root Chakra and ending with the Throat Chakra. While the Third Eye Chakra and the Crown Chakra are not located in the spinal column itself they still follow the same central axis. There are a few theories regarding the scientific nature of these two chakras, and it is worth examining two of the main ones. First, there is the theory that the sixth and seventh chakras are related to the pineal and the pituitary glands. In the case of the sixth or the Third Eye Chakra, the pineal gland is seen as the corresponding energy center. The significance of this is that the pineal gland is responsible for creating melatonin which regulates sleep patterns. Since the third eye is considered the subconscious mind in many traditions it is profoundly significant that the Third Eye Chakra would be located in a place where sleep, and thus dreams are regulated. Many ancient traditions view dreams as the realm of the subconscious, equally real and important to physical reality. The idea that the ancients placed the seat of the intellect and subconscious mind in the same vicinity as the pineal gland has to be far more than mere coincidence.

Physicians and philosophers alike have attributed the pineal gland with such things as the intellect and even the soul itself.

René Descartes was a world-renowned scientist and philosopher in the sixteen hundreds. He wrote several books on anatomy and the soul, two of which dealt with the pineal gland in particular. According to Descartes, the pineal gland was where our soul resided and was the very place where all thoughts originated. While modern science is still struggling to understand the complexities of the human brain it might be time to consider the patterns already emerging. The fact that the pineal gland is responsible for sleep, and thus dreams, and that some prominent thinkers have attributed it to the center of thought and the subconscious self, coupled with the fact that the Third Eye Chakra is located in the same region, should be enough to convince anyone that these assertions are in fact true. Again, this is just one more example of where the physical body closely mirrors the dynamics of the subtle body.

The Crown Chakra, or the seventh chakra, is the highest chakra of the seven. Located at the crown of the head, it resides between the physical body and the realm beyond. One theory links this chakra with the pituitary gland, which makes a lot of sense when you understand the functions of the pituitary gland. The main function of the pituitary gland is to produce and secrete hormones—chemicals that affect functions throughout the rest of the body. Some of the functions affected by the hormones produced by the pituitary gland include Thyroid function, water absorption, and regulation of temperature, pain and pain relief, regulation of blood pressure, growth, and sex organ functions. All in all, the pituitary gland can be seen as a controller of just about every facet of the physical body's function and wellbeing. In a way, the pituitary gland is like the conductor of an orchestra, overseeing that every member of the orchestra performs their part exactly as it ought to be performed. Is it any wonder that this is where the chakra associated with a higher being is located? After all, what function does the Higher Being have than to oversee and regulate the function of all life? Again, is it mere coincidence that the chakral centers have been placed where they have, or is modern science simply revealing that the wisdom of the ancients is, in fact, accurate and deserves greater attention and respect?

The association of the sixth and seventh chakras with the pineal and pituitary glands is just one theory which serves to confirm the validity of the chakral tradition. Another theory which deserves attention is the one that focuses on the general regions of the Third Eye and Crown Chakras. This theory doesn't focus on specific glands, but rather it focuses on the area of the brain and the top of the head. In the case of the sixth or Third Eye Chakra, the location of this chakra is basically in the forehead region, which is where the brain itself is largely located. Again, this has great significance as the brain is scientifically known to be the seat of all thought, emotions and even dreams, thus it can be considered the seat of the subconscious. While this is nothing new in terms of our understanding of the human condition, it should be noted that different cultures throughout history viewed things quite differently. The ancient Greeks, for example, saw various organs as the seat of the soul, including the heart, liver and even the abdomen. In fact, the Greeks believed that the lower organs were the originators of emotional joy and or pain.

That said, the notion that the brain is the center of thought, creativity, and even the subconscious is, in fact, a very recent one. Only within the last few hundred years has the seat of the mind found its way to the head. Thus, the fact that the ancient Indian sages placed the chakra responsible for intellect and wisdom in the forehead was far more than mere luck. Again, due to the primitive science and technology available at the time it is hard to imagine that the placement of the Third Eye Chakra had anything to do with a deeper understanding of human anatomy and physiology. Rather, it seems that by understanding the workings and design of a person's subtle body the ancients were able to lay the foundations for a more accurate and in-depth understanding of the workings and design of the physical body.

The Crown Chakra is a bit of a mystery in terms of its location on the human body. Depending on the tradition you read, this chakra is located at or just above the crown of a person's head. In terms of spiritual significance, this makes perfect sense as the Crown Chakra is literally your connection to the higher realm of spirit. In a sense you could relate the Crown Chakra to the leaves on a tree, existing between the tree itself and the air all around it. And, just as the leaves of a tree absorb the energy from the air and the sun, so too, the Crown Chakra absorbs the energy from the higher realms. Still, this doesn't really do much for proving that the ancients had some advanced understanding of how the physical body worked as a result of their insights regarding the subtle body. That is unless you consider a concept that is gaining more and more acceptance within the scientific community. This concept is the one regarding auras. The aura of a person is literally an envelope of energy that radiates from and surrounds the person. Recent advances in photographic and electromagnetic technology have enabled us to actually see the human aura for the first time in recorded history. And this phenomenon has gone a long way to changing our understanding of how energy affects life overall.

While a person's aura envelops their whole body, the most

visible elements of it are around the head. Thus, the virtual energy of a person can be seen just above their shoulders and above the crown of their head. This is where the ancient symbol of the halo comes to mind. When we think of a halo we are reminded of the holiest people, or angels or deities themselves. Additionally, while halos are normally associated with Christianity, the fact of the matter is that they have representations throughout many traditions across many different times and places throughout history. Thus, while the traditions themselves may differ, the association of halos with purity or divinity remains constant. Furthermore, the more divine or holy a person was, the larger and brighter their halo was. Suddenly we have our physical connection with the location of the seventh chakra. The Crown Chakra—that which connects a person with the divine, is in the same place as the energy 'crown' of a person's physical body. And, just as this energy crown lingers on and just above the head, so too the Crown Chakra does the same. Due to the realization that our physical body has an energy envelope of sorts, our representation of the human form may have to be changed from its current physical only form to one which incorporates its energy aspect as well.

The fact that modern science has discovered energy centers in the same locations as for where the ancients placed the seven main chakras is nothing short of extraordinary. Even the harshest skeptic would have to take a moment to consider the significance of what this actually means. However, in case you thought that this was the only correlation between the chakral traditions and modern science, rest assured, there is more! The chakras and the nerve centers are described as focal points for energy. This energy was seen as the electrical communications between the brain and the body and nothing more for many years. However, modern breakthroughs in the fields of electromagnetism and quantum physics have led to yet more correlations between modern science and ancient wisdom. Modern research has begun to determine that not all energy is the same. Just as radio waves exist on different frequencies, so too, energy can exist in different forms. The variations of energy are often referred to in terms of vibrations. Lower vibrations create different forms of energy than higher vibrations. In fact, it is theorized that matter itself is merely energy on a really low vibrational frequency. This is the basis of all teleportation theories. Converting matter to energy is not as difficult as it once seemed since matter itself is now seen as a level of energy. Still, how does this relate to chakras? Simply put, science is now realizing that the human body does, in fact, absorb energy from its surroundings as well as from the food that it ingests.

Once science realized that electromagnetic energy is all around us, moving past us and even through us at all times, the question was raised as to how this energy affected us. On the physiological level, certain energies can, in fact, be dangerous. People who live or work near areas with high electromagnetic activity often contract cancers and other ailments, now being linked to the high concentrations of energy. There has also been an association of energy and mood, suggesting that a person's mind can be directly influenced by the energy in the environment. At first, this doesn't make sense since energy, like radio waves, needs a receiver in order to be of any actual value. And, just like a radio, the human body would need to convert the energy received into usable information. Simply receiving the radio waves is not enough for a radio to play music. A radio must convert those radio waves back into vibrations in order to produce the appropriate sounds. Here we find two distinct correlations to chakral energy and wellbeing.

The first correlation is in terms of the chakras acting as energy centers. By understanding that energy flows around us and through us at all times, these centers take on a whole new meaning. Not only do they generate energy that flows through our physical and subtle bodies, affecting our overall health and wellbeing, but they also receive energy from the environment. This means that they absorb as well as generate energy. Thus, when a chakra is closed or damaged its ability to absorb useful energy is significantly reduced. This is like not being able to digest food properly. It is no wonder, in light of this, that damaged chakras can so significantly reduce a person's health and wellbeing. The importance of having healthy, vibrant chakras is therefore even more critical as the health of our chakras determines our ability to take in energy.

The second correlation is in terms of vibration. Ancient chakral traditions are filled with references to the various vibrations related to each chakra, and how those vibrations can increase the health and vitality of each particular chakra. Mantras are the number one tool for creating the necessary vibration pattern in order to invigorate a weakened chakra. The fact that energy exists at different vibrational wavelengths only confirms the validity of chakral wisdom. Why else would the ancients have been aware of the importance of different vibrations unless they understood the relationship between vibrations and energy? Thus, the next time you begin to feel self-conscious when you are chanting a mantra in order to revitalize the energies of a particular chakra, realize that what you are doing is in fact scientifically proven.

Another important concept to consider is that of the different types of energy and their effects on a person. Just as different sounds invoke different feelings, so too, different energies can do the same. Since energy is all around us at all times it is no wonder that a person can experience different moods throughout the day for seemingly no reason. Additionally, the notion that different energies have different frequencies can go a long way to explaining why we can feel good around some people and uncomfortable around others. The fact that a person takes in and generates energy means that you can feel a person's nature just by being around them. Since most people focus on a specific range of energy, just like a radio tunes in to a specific frequency, they will radiate the same feelings day in and day out. This means that when you get a bad feeling about someone, despite the fact that they are being kind to you, you should protect yourself from that person. Additionally, when you get a feeling about a person you don't even know, you should trust that feeling implicitly. The fact is that each person attracts and radiates the energies of the frequency they are tuned into. Thus, negative people will draw in and put out negative energy, which will make you feel uneasy. Alternatively, positive people will attract and generate energy that makes you feel good and safe.

CHAPTER 20:

AS ABOVE, SO BELOW

When you are dealing with a topic as sacred and as vital as that of chakras it is hard to determine which points are the most important. The more you look at each and every detail is the more you realize how critical all of those details are. Even so, there are some aspects of chakral wisdom which seem to stand just a bit more than all the rest. One such aspect is that the subtle body and the physical body are completely interrelated. The health and wellbeing of the one translate directly to the health and wellbeing of the other. This sense of symbiosis is perhaps the very cornerstone of all chakral wisdom. After all, only by knowing how the chakras impact your body can you know their actual condition. Additionally, all of the methods for improving chakral health invariably involve physical action of one form or another. Thus, while the subtle and physical bodies may be seen as separate entities, it is perhaps a mistake to view them as such. Rather, they should be seen as two sides of a single coin. You cannot alter the one without affecting the other.

While the symbiotic nature of the subtle and physical bodies may not be new to some people, it can open a door to many insights that actually may be unfamiliar to most. One of these insights is the idea that you can develop health both from the outside in and from the inside out. This knowledge will not only help you to understand what physical actions can help to heal chakral energies, but it can also reveal what physical conditions are in fact harmful to your chakras in the first place. By knowing which environments and conditions to avoid in order to maintain good chakral health you will be able to protect yourself, much the same way as you can protect your physical health by avoiding unhealthy foods and the like. After all, the adage 'an ounce of prevention is worth a pound of cure' is no less applicable to chakral health as it is to anything else. Thus, knowing what to avoid will go a long way to maintaining chakral health and wellbeing and will keep you from having to take extra steps to restore vital chakral energies.

The first thing to recognize is the absolute importance of emotions. When you consider emotions they can tend to be a bit of an enigma. On the one hand, emotions are seen as non-physical products of the heart or the mind. This makes sense as you cannot go out and buy a pound of happiness at the grocery store. However, to simply classify emotions as non-physical is to miss the other side of their importance. The truth of the matter is that emotions have a very real impact on our physical wellbeing. When you are happy and free of stress your physical body will be more energetic and healthy overall. Alternatively, when you are anxious and depressed your physical body will lack vitality and will be more prone to sickness and disease. While this is nothing new, what is often not considered is the significance of this dynamic. If an emotion is non-physical then it must be classified as energy. That said, as energy, it must be generated and governed by energy centers. And, as you have learned by now, the energy centers in a person are what are called *chakras*. Thus, emotions can be seen as the bridge between the physical and the subtle bodies of any individual.

The question now is how does knowing the importance of emotions help in maintaining chakral health and wellbeing? The answer to this lies in redefining what an emotion truly is. Generally speaking, emotions are seen as how you feel about a certain thing or another. If you like your job, then you will be happy at your job. If you like a particular person, then you will be happy to be with that person. In fact, you may be so happy being with that particular person that you might seek to share your life with them in a more significant way. Alternatively, if you don't like your job, or you don't like a person, then you will feel uneasy and even unhappy as a result. Being at work will drain all of your energy, and being with that person will make you anxious and even depressed. As true as this is, it only addresses the surface value of what emotions actually are. The fact of the matter is that emotions can be seen as a compass of sorts. By knowing what makes you happy and what makes you sad, you can steer a course that avoids unhappiness and takes you to things that help to improve how you feel.

Again, it is important to recognize the fact that emotions are energy. Once you truly understand that point the rest will become increasingly clear. Energy, as we have discussed, operates on different vibrations or frequencies. Positive energy will thus operate on a different frequency than negative energy. Since your subtle body is comprised of energy, and your chakras are the energy centers responsible for receiving and processing energy, then your emotions can be seen as a virtual meter, determining the type of energy that surrounds us at any given time. Rather than being a mere reaction to something, now your emotional response to things can be seen as a form of communication from your chakras themselves. Essentially, your emotions are the language of your subtle body! Once you realize this truth then the full significance of your emotional state becomes very clear. Positive emotions are your chakras telling you that the environment you are in is pleasant and desirable, and this should encourage you to spend as much time in that environment as you can. Negative emotions, however, are your chakras telling you that the environment or circumstances you are in are unpleasant and that you should remove yourself to another place as quickly as possible.

Needless to say, removing yourself from an unpleasant environment or situation may often be easier said than done. This is especially true in the event that you have a job that you don't particularly like. Simply getting up and walking out of your unpleasant job may seem like a fantasy worth fulfilling, however, the truth of the matter is that you would probably regret it as soon as you walked out the door. No matter how bad a job is, it is far better than having no job at all, especially if you rely on the money that it provides. In the case where you are forced to endure a negative environment on a regular basis, it is critical to making sure that you take the necessary steps to decompress from that environment as often as possible. Whether you choose to go to a place that makes you extremely happy, or whether you choose to simply perform yoga or meditation to purify your chakras when you get home, the important thing is that you take steps to counterbalance the harmful impact that any negative environment has on your chakral energies. The last thing that you want to do is to allow yourself to be controlled by the negative energies that surround you at a particular place that you cannot free yourself from.

Another aspect of emotional response to consider is how dangerous the philosophy of adaptation can actually be. Many people argue that the key to survival is to overcome your fears or other emotional negativity to a particular situation and simply accept that situation as the way things are. In the case of a job you don't like, if you adopt this philosophy you will wind up suppressing your emotional response to the environment, thus allowing yourself to be exposed to harmful energy on a daily basis for no good reason. Since emotions are the language of your subtle form they should always be trusted. Furthermore, your emotional response to a particular thing should never be suppressed or ignored. Adaptation, therefore, while it may seem appealing is actually very harmful overall. It is one thing to accept a situation until you are able to change it, as this will reduce your stress levels significantly. However, to accept a negative situation indefinitely is nothing short of self-destructive behavior. The ideal response to any negative situation or environment is to remove yourself from it as soon as possible. If you don't like your job, begin looking for a different job. Make every effort to find another job so that you can place yourself in a more positive environment, one which will benefit your chakral energies rather than drain them.

The importance of placing yourself where your energies are happy cannot be overstated. In short, this is the difference between surviving and thriving. While adapting to a situation can be seen as the key to survival, improving your situation is the key to thriving. If you study life carefully you will notice that survival is not the be all and end all. Quite the opposite, survival is merely the absolute minimum needed to not die. The goal of nature, and thus all life, is to do more than merely not die. It becomes clear the more you observe life that the Universe truly intends for each and every one of us to thrive. Therefore, your emotional reaction to certain environments or conditions isn't a matter of judgment as such, rather it is an indicator that the environment or condition at hand is not ideal for your personal design. Since each person is unique, it makes sense that everyone needs a slightly different set of circumstances in order to thrive. Your emotions are the way in which your higher self, or your subtle form, directs you to the conditions that are suited specifically for your wellbeing. Therefore, to follow your emotions is to follow the divine roadmap that will lead to the environment where you can benefit the most and reach your true potential.

Needless to say, the significance of positive energy is as applicable to people as it is to places or circumstances. Whenever you find yourself in the company of people who are negative or who have a negative impact on your emotions you will find that your energies are soured at best, and completely drained at worst. In the event that you can remove yourself from the company of such people, then that, of course, is what you should do. The idea that you should have endless compassion or sympathy for people who cause you emotional harm has its place, but not at your personal expense. You can love people you don't particularly like from a safe distance. There is no rule that says you need to expose yourself to their negative energies indefinitely. However, in the case where you cannot simply remove yourself from the company of negative energy people, such as at work, then you need to make sure that you take the time to perform the previously mentioned methods for chakral energy restoration. Again, the last thing you need is to be controlled by the negative energies that you are necessarily subjected to on a regular basis.

While negative emotions can serve as a warning to help you avoid the negative energies that would harm you, so too, positive emotions will show you the places and people who will serve to increase your overall happiness and wellbeing. Once you discover these sources of positive energy it should be your goal to place yourself in those environments or to surround yourself with those people as often as possible. In the case of a location, when you find a place that restores your chakral energies you should make it a habit to frequent that place as often as possible. Such a place doesn't have to be mystical in nature, such as a majestic mountaintop or a tranquil lake, rather it can take any form at all. For some people, a museum might provide the perfect environment for restoring their chakral energies, whereas for others it might be a favorite coffee shop or a bookstore. The appearance and form of the place itself don't matter at all. What truly matters is the effect that the place has on your energies. When you discover a place that has a restorative effect on your chakral energies you need to go there on a regular basis. In the event that it is a coffee shop or a bookstore, you might even consider trying to get a job there, although that is a move that can backfire quickly if you aren't careful. After all, trading in a place to escape from a place of work can take away the restorative nature of the place and leave you without a place to escape to. In any event, be sure to make use of the place as often as you can.

People can have a similar restorative effect on your chakral energies as well. Sometimes this can take the form of particular friends, whereas in other cases it might take the form of social groups. The popularity of churches, for example, can more often than not be explained in these terms. If you talk to people who regularly attend church you will discover that the social dynamic of the church is what they benefit from the most. Any religious setting can have a profound impact on your chakral energy as it can offer a place where people of like mind, and thus like energies, can be found. The significance of the energy that you take in from other people cannot be overstated. Just as being around people you don't like can drain and damage your energies, so too, being around people you do like can restore and invigorate your chakral energies and overall wellbeing. Thus, you should seek out people that make you happy regardless of who they are. Again, just as the appearance and form of your safe place aren't important, the identity of the people who make you happy isn't important either. What is important is that you follow the lead of your emotions, as this is the direction your subtle form is giving you.

Finding the people and places that restore and strengthen your chakral energies is one of the most important things you can do for your overall sense of health and wellbeing, since as your energies are restored, so too, your physical body will be restored as well. The trap that so many people fall into is that they feel that rest and rest alone is what restores drained energy. While rest is important, surrounding yourself with positive energy is equally important. By relying too heavily on solitude and rest you can actually rob yourself of many energy restorative options, thereby starving yourself of some much needed positive energy. Since places and people contain and generate energy, surrounding yourself with the right places and people is the same as eating the right foods. In essence, energy is the food of the subtle body. Thus, just as the physical body derives energy from the food it consumes, the subtle body derives energy from the energy it is exposed to. Therefore, spending enough time in happy places and with happy people is just as important as eating enough of the right foods.

In the end, the important thing to understand is how much our day to day lives impact our spiritual wellbeing. When you live a life dominated by negative people, places, and events, then your chakral energies will be depleted and distressed. This will result in your physical body being deprived of energy and vitality, causing you to feel fatigued and to be in generally poor health. However, when you live a life dominated by positive people, places, and events, then your chakral energies will be positive and vibrant. This will result in your physical body being energized and healthy, creating an overall sense of vitality and wellbeing. This symbiotic relationship between the physical and the subtle bodies shows how everything you do affects both aspects of your person equally. Thus, the key to happiness and spiritual health lies in your commitment to pursuing those things that bring you happiness and contentment, and thus, serve to restore and maintain your spiritual and physical health and wellbeing.

CONCLUSION

Thank you again for reading this book!

I hope this book was able to help you to cleanse and balance your chakras.

The next step is to recharge your home with all the energies of love and life.

Finally, if you enjoyed this book, then I'd like to ask you for a favor, would you be kind enough to leave a review for this book on Amazon? I would **really appreciate it!**

Simply go to **bit.ly/chakrareview** to leave a review for this book on Amazon.

I would love for you to connect with me on Social Media with any questions, comments or just to experience beautiful images and inspirational quotes.

Amazing Instagram: **@Yogitation**
Website: www.qualitychapters.com

Thank you and good luck,

Michael Williams

Don't forget to get your FREE Bonus Gift!

Thanks again for taking your time to read my book. I would also want you to continue on your path to a more peaceful and enjoyable life, therefore I'm going to give you the **"Yoga For All: The Simple Guide To Yoga & Meditation"** e-book for FREE!

Go to **bit.ly/freebookyoga** to download the FREE e-book.

Preview of Buddhism:

Beginner's Guide to Understanding & Practicing Buddhism to Become Stress and Anxiety Free

INTRODUCTION

Do you know that Buddhism is more popular now than it was half a century ago?

You can tell, based on the surge of books written about it as well as the increase in the number of Buddhist and Yoga schools, throughout the globe, notably in the west. You might even have noticed more people – from movie stars to athletes, your next-door neighbor to millionaire tycoons – that are incorporating such Buddhist practices as meditation into their everyday life.

However, many of the common questions about Buddhism remain unanswered. For instance, is it some sort of religion with its own rigid set of rules? Is it a carefree type of lifestyle? What is reincarnation? Is karma similar to fate?

If you are curious to know the answers, and if you want to learn more about Buddhism, especially with regard to becoming stress- and anxiety-free, then this book was written especially for you!

It is no secret that Buddhism is a complex topic. After all, the seed that the First Buddha planted almost three thousand years ago is now a massive tree that continues to branch out to this day. Nevertheless, this book can help you build a strong foundation for learning and practicing Buddhism.

All the fundamental questions asked by beginners are answered here, such as what Buddhism is and what its teachings are. Core subjects such as the Four Noble Truths and the Noble Eightfold Path are described clearly. Buddhist concepts such as Reincarnation, Nirvana, and Karma are also explained in a clear and concise way. Theories aside, you will also learn the practical side of Buddhism, specifically to help you achieve peace and relaxation each day.

This book is for anybody who is curious about Buddhism, particularly those who are considering it as their guide to a happy and purposeful life.

Now, the choice is yours. Clear the fog and begin your spiritual journey towards attaining peace of mind and clarity. The First Chapter awaits you!

A MIND UNPERTURBED BY THE VAGARIES OF FORTUNE, FROM SORROW, FREED, FROM DEFILEMENTS CLEANSED, FROM FEAR LIBERATED - THIS IS THE GREATEST BLESSING

CHAPTER 1

WHAT IS BUDDHISM?

"A mind unperturbed by the vagaries of fortune, from sorrow freed, from defilements cleansed, from fear liberated — this is the greatest blessing."

– The Buddha

Hello! You must be the kind of person who is eager to learn new things every day. After all, why else would you choose this book?

You must be curious about Buddhism. You might have heard of it from somewhere, such as on social media or from a friend who is passionate about its teachings.

You might also have heard about the many ways it has helped those who find their true purpose in life, or – at the

185

very least – find peace and calm in the midst of a seemingly fast-paced and stressful world.

A million questions might be swimming in your brain concerning Buddhism. In a while, they will be answered.

First, do take comfort in being here right now: reading this book and acquiring the knowledge that can help you find true happiness in everyday life.

One of the most essential teachings of Buddhism is an understanding that where you are at this moment is exactly where you are intended to be. As each moment passes, you are following your own course throughout life and enjoying and taking in each moment is paramount in creating a path of wisdom and understanding for yourself. Revel in each and every sentence, taking the time to fully understand what you are reading because in Buddhism every tale, every reading, and every teaching pave the way to more open, joyful, and enlightened path in life.

Look around you and notice how your body has naturally kept you alive. Your lungs continue to breathe without you having to tell it to do so. Your eyelids blink automatically to keep your eyes moist and protected. Your blood continues to flow underneath your skin, oblivious to your surroundings and thoughts.

Also, notice how you are able to comprehend the words on this page. Is that not something to be grateful? Take a moment to consider this thought.

Are you still here? Hopefully yes, because now let us answer what may be the first question in your mind: What is Buddhism?

What is Buddhism?

Would it surprise you to know that Buddhism is not a religion? At least, not in the sense wherein it is an institution that dictates how one should believe in a divine power.

In fact, there is no deity to be worshipped, although you might wonder why some seem to be worshipping the statues of the Buddha. While there indeed are those who worship his image (and erroneously so), true Buddhists merely pay respect to the memory of the Buddha. They neither worship nor pray to him. The Buddha himself is a guide and teacher for those that seek the path to enlightenment.

Many people who wake up each morning with the intention of practicing Buddhist teachings find inspiration from the gentle image of the Buddha. It is not unlike finding your motivation from the words of a successful person. His peaceful and meditative image can help you understand and remember the teachings you are following when life becomes stressful, and your mind begins to run off course.

Buddhism is a way of life that leads to the discernment of true reality. Its teachings center on developing your ability to be mindful of your thoughts, actions, and surroundings. All these lead to a life that is in tune with nature and your true self.

The practices of Buddhism – including meditation and yoga – are meant to help you unlearn your preconceived notions of yourself and the world. They serve as your guide towards embracing such qualities as kindness, love, true wisdom, and awareness.

Those who continually walk the path of Buddhism usually find themselves achieving the state of "perfect enlightenment."

In other words, they become a "Buddha." A Buddha is a being who has been able to see the nature of life as it truly is. The enlightened being then continues to live life fully, all the while upholding the principles that are in line with this vision.

The idea of enlightenment can be broken down into two simple forms, the mind, and the self. The mind is that constant voice that has been molded and constructed based on the world around you in this life. Self is that inner being that is separate from the meat of your body and does not change based on any teachings or experiences that life brings you. Your real self is what can be understood to travel from life to life during reincarnation.

Each and every living being has the opportunity to become enlightened in each life they live. There is no set course or prewritten script for your life. As discussed later in this book, Karma plays a part in deciding the circumstances in which you will be born into from life to life, but your own spiritual and mental ambition are what drives each person to take one step closer to full enlightenment.

However, things get interesting here, because when you follow the path of Buddhism, you do not have an "end goal." It is a paradox for one to declare that they are going to practice Buddhism in order to reach enlightenment.

Who is The Buddha?

The word "Buddha" translates to "the enlightened one" or "the awakened being." It refers to any being who has achieved this state. However, you might be curious to know about the first Buddha.

According to legend, the first Buddha was named Siddhartha Gautama. Many believe that he was born around 563 B.C. in a land that is now found in Nepal. It is said that The Buddha was born a royal, shielded from the suffering of the kingdom of his father, who built a grand palace around him void of religion or human suffering. The King created an entire world inside those castle walls and, as he grew, led him to believe that the world was one of happiness, empathy, and joy. Later in his life, after he had married and was raised, he ventured out into the world and saw the truth of humanity. He met an old man and found that all people age, and eventually die.

At the age of twenty-nine, he found that neither his power nor his fortune brought him true happiness, and he wanted to understand the world outside of the palace walls.

Therefore, what he did was he set out to explore as many religions across the world to find the answer to the question that we all ask ourselves, "Where can one find happiness?"

Several years into his spiritual pilgrimage, the Buddha discovered "The Middle Path" while meditating under the Bodhi tree. This path is a way of balance, not of extremism, which he found only through trial and error. He sat for days under that Bodhi tree seeking the answers he had initially set out to find. During this meditation, Siddhartha had to face the evil demon known as Mara, who threatened to stand in the way of his Buddha status. He looked to the earth for guidance and the land answered by banishing Mara and allowing Siddhartha to reach full enlightenment. Such discernments led him to achieve the perfect state of enlightenment. After this life-changing experience, the Buddha then lived the rest of his days sharing what he discovered. The followers of the Buddha's teachings called his principles the *Dharma*, or "Truth."

It is thought that Buddha, or anyone who reaches the state of perfect enlightenment in their lifetime, no longer continues on the circle of rebirth. Instead, the Buddha is thought to sit outside of constant reincarnation and sends teachings and guidance to those searching for their own freedom of self. They no longer have to sit through what Buddhists believe to be an endless cycle of suffering known as life.

When you hear the word suffering, you may have images of pain and anger, come into your mind, but in Buddhism, they believe that all life is suffering. As humans, we feel the pain of loss, the emotions of sadness, happiness, disappointment, and so on. These emotions are manifestations of our mind, and they do not come from our inner selves. Because they do not come from our true self, they are thought of as suffering. False feelings created by the meat of our brains, programmed into us by what our societal view has taught.

Currently, Buddhism is increasingly becoming a popular way of life for millions of people, across the world. Even those in the Western countries seek to follow The Middle Path because they find that it speaks to their heart.

In a world where everything is always in motion, constantly forcing us to move forward at a quicker and more rapid pace, many people feel the loss of their connection with nature. Though nature is all around us, even, in the major cities, what we have done to change the pure form of earth, creates a disconnect from our minds. In Buddhism, you are connected to every natural thing in this world, and by practicing the teachings of it, you are brought back to that connection. This is an enormous draw for millions of people all over the world. You can think of it as connecting back to your roots.

Another reason why Buddhism is widespread is the fact that the Buddha never claimed to be a god. Instead, he was a teacher who shared his wisdom based on his own discernment and experiences in life. This lack of an invisible deity often speaks to those that cannot find solace or belief in other religions where God is their governing body. Though there are many tales and teachings in Buddhism, there is no one holy book such as a Bible or Quran. Instead, the "bible" of Buddhism can be found in every natural effect on the planet, from the leaves on the trees to the worms in the ground. They are the story of the past, but you don't need to look to the past to find enlightenment, you need to look at every moment that you experience.

Moreover, the belief system of Buddhism is one that can be described as "large-minded." This means that those who practice it are open to accepting the moral teachings of other belief systems. Therefore, they are unconcerned with labels that pertain to specific religions, such as "Catholic," "Baptist," "Hindu," "Muslim," or even "Buddhist" itself. It is not uncommon to find those of different religious background meditating together at various Buddhist centers, especially in the western world. Enlightenment, in Buddhism, is not based on who you believe created you, but rather by opening your mind enough to allow yourself to shine through. Once that is reached, all the answers you seek on creation will be known to you. Therefore, your title of faith is of no concern, though, those that strive for enlightenment do usually find themselves identifying as Buddhist or other similar namesakes.

Buddhists neither seek an expansion of an organization, nor attempt to convince others of a certain belief. Instead, they only provide an explanation if asked. The Buddha encourages one to be curious through awareness; therefore, Buddhism can be regarded more as a way of life based on discernment rather than faith.

191

Though Buddhism as a practice can bend and move on a scale depending on your dedication to the teachings and heritage, anyone can practice the Buddhist way of living. There is always an extreme importance put on the word empathy, throughout the teachings of Buddhas through the generations. Empathy is not just reserved for humans, but for every living creature of this world.

At this point, you must be eager to learn the different teachings of the Buddha. Keep in mind that the Buddha's teachings are vast to such an extent that it grew into many different types of Buddhism. These teachings can bring wisdom to anyone, whether seeking to find their true self through enlightenment, or those that just wish to understand the world around them a little bit better. These teachings are for the young and old alike, regardless of religion, status, gender, or heritage.

However, let us not get ahead of ourselves. For now, you can explore more about the teachings of Buddhism, which you can conveniently find in the next chapter. Before you do turn the page, though, please do remember the advice of the Buddha himself. It is to take care not to take his word for it but to test for yourself his teachings. Only by doing so would you then be able to find the true meaning of his words.

To check out the rest of the book, simply search for the title below on Amazon or go to:

bit.ly/Buddhism2

Buddhism: Beginner's Guide to Understanding & Practicing Buddhism to Become Stress and Anxiety Free

Check Out My Other Books

Below you'll find my other books that are popular on Amazon and Kindle as well. Simply enter the name of the books in the search bar on Amazon to check them out. Alternatively, you can visit my author page on Amazon to see other work done by me.

- *Michael Williams' Author Page on Amazon*
- *Buddhism:* *Beginner's Guide to Understanding & Practicing Buddhism to Become Stress and Anxiety Free*

- *Buddhism For Beginners - How To Go From Beginner To Monk And Master Your Mind*

- **ZEN:** *Beginner's Guide to Understanding & Practicing Zen Meditation to Become Present*

- ***Yoga For Men:*** *Beginner's Step by Step Guide to a Stronger Body & Sharper Mind*

- ***Chakras for Beginners*** *- Awaken Your Internal Energy and Learn to Radiate Positive Energy and Start Healing*

195

- **Mindfulness for Beginners** – *How to Live in The Present, Stress, and Anxiety Free*

- **Mindfulness:** *An Eight-Step Guide to Finding Peace and Removing Negativity From Your Everyday Life*

- **Mindfulness For Beginners** – *How to Relieve Stress and Anxiety Like a Buddhist Monk and Live In the Present Moment In Your Everyday Life*

- **Empath:** *How to Stop Worrying and Eliminate Negative Thinking as a Sensitive Person*

Made in the USA
Middletown, DE
07 November 2018